MW01037137

The Abba
FACTOR

Dr. Kerry Wood
with Dr. Chiqui Wood

Original Print Version
Copyright © 2018 Kerry Wood
ISBN: 978-1-940359-61-8
Library of Congress Number: 2018932482
Published in the United States of America

All rights reserved as permitted under the U. S. Copyright Act of 1976. No part of this publication may be reproduced, distributed, or transmitted in any form or by any means, or stored in a database or retrieval system, without the expressed written permission of the author and publisher.

Unless otherwise marked, Scripture quotations are taken from the New King James Version® (NKJV). Copyright © 1982 by Thomas Nelson. Used by permission. All rights reserved.

Scripture quotations marked NIV are taken from THE HOLY BIBLE, NEW INTERNATIONAL VERSION®, NIV® Copyright © 1973, 1978, 1984, 2011 by Biblica, Inc.® Used by permission. All rights reserved worldwide.

Scripture quotations marked MSG are taken from The Message. Copyright © 1993, 1994, ¹995, 1996, 2000, 2001, 2002 by Eugene H. Peterson.

Scripture quotations marked AMP are taken from the Amplified Bible. Copyright © 1954, 1958, 1962, 1964, 1965, 1987 by The Lockman Foundation

Cover Design: Ivethe Zambrano-Fernández
wwwdesignbytwo.com

Photography of Author by John Choate

Bedford, Texas
www.BurkhartBooks.com

Dedication and Acknowledgments

I dedicate this book to Chiqui, my adorable, loving, and brilliant wife. Thank you for prodding me forward to write, giving wise input, and making my life more heaven on earth than any man deserves.

Thanks to The King's University, Southlake, Texas, for inviting me to teach these truths in a summer intensive in 2017, especially Cole Barnett, Rachel Clark, Chloe Dwyer, Allen Powers, Taren Walters, and Lauren Waltz—students at The King's—who invested considerable time reading, listening, and giving honest feedback in the writing process.

Thanks to Ryan Northcutt, Phil and Beth Strickland, and my wife Chiqui, for their feedback and editing skills. You will want to obtain the companions to this first of three in a trilogy by Chiqui and me. The second is *The Abba Foundation* (Dr. Chiqui Wood's theological foundations to everything I offer in the other two volumes) and the third is *The Abba Formation* (a deep dive into how the Holy Spirit downloads our new identity and processes our transformation as revealed in 1 Corinthians, Chapter Two). Her volume is critical because we can connect the sonship and orphan ideas in wrong ways if we don't have an accurate view of the nature of the Father. Sonship, after all, is all about how we relate to the Father.

Finally, many thanks to Todd and Tammy Williams for their generosity in sharing their luxurious cabin, Twelve Stones (Broken Bow, OK), as our writing haven—I'm not sure how long it would have taken to finish this without such a refuge.

Contents

Preface

I'm forever grateful for my spiritual upbringing—my parents loved God fervently and passed that spiritual heritage on to their children. We were in church three times per week. But there was something not quite right that I didn't understand as a child. Many years ago, mind you, my father (one of the hardest working, most godly men I have ever known), continually shrank back under pressure. I didn't understand why he would run from conflict. Numerous times I saw him walk out the door, get in his car and drive away to avoid working through some family situation with my mom.

Of course, I didn't see this as strange at the time—it's just the way it was in our home. It was our "normal." But as I grew older I began to wonder why. I remember feelings of both resentment and pity and wanted my dad to be strong and brave. I resented him running instead of staying to work things out. I also remember feeling sorry for him, pitying him, and feeling anger towards mom or anyone else whom I thought was causing him pain.

Then my siblings and I slowly began to hear stories about Dad being orphaned as a two-year-old child in the Depression years. It is difficult to understand now, but there was a time in America when some families only had two options: either let the children starve or put them in an orphanage until things got better. In my father's case, he and his siblings were put in an orphanage. In a twist of divine providence (in my view) Dad was adopted out to a Christian family and separated from his siblings until his twenties.

Though he was raised in a Christian home in a way that his biological siblings weren't, the separation left an indelible mark on my father. I was in my late thirties before I began to see a connection between Dad's conflict-avoidance and a lingering orphan mentality.

This subject is more than a preaching or teaching topic; it is part of the terrain of my life, the journey of my own soul, and the fabric of my family. I write and speak passionately about this topic because it is my life message. More about that, if you will allow, in the pages to come.

"I Think He Said This Before"

My students often hear me say, "*I have been delivered from the fear of repetition.*" There are some truths that need to be repeated many times over and said in as many different ways as possible. Herein, be forewarned that I will say some things multiple times and multiple ways, intentionally.

This is both to lodge a truth as deeply into the heart and mind of a hearer as possible, but also to help the learner "connect the dots"—to make the application of that truth to multiple facets of your life and understanding. I ask that you humbly receive it again and again, like a tender plant that needs daily watering. I know I need it continually. Please walk with me on a journey of discovery—I am still in the throes of this discovery, as Paul said, "to apprehend that which has apprehended me."

A Necessary Humility

I approach this task of writing about *The Abba Factor*—the Holy Spirit's role in facilitating intimacy and spiritual transformation—with a certain sense of fear and trepidation. I have grown up around the things of the Spirit, and I am sure that it has both sensitized and de-sensitized me in ways in which I am unaware. My constant conversation with God is that I do not speak as if I have this all figured out; not even remotely close. Jesus said of the Holy Spirit, "The wind blows where it wants to; no one understands where it comes from or where it is going. In the same way, the Holy Spirit ..." (John 3:8). If Jesus, in union and constant communion with the Father and Spirit would say this, what do we really know about Him?

And yet, He has revealed Himself to us (through a glass darkly) to draw us to Himself. He wants us to know Him, and we can know God through Jesus Christ by the Spirit. As Church history reveals, to shrug our shoulders and say, "It's too far beyond us to bother inquiry and conversation with God," is first of all to forget that God invites us to know Him, and secondly, that we have a responsibility, at His behest, to partner with Him to see the nations streaming into Zion. So, we must welcome God's invitation that:

I will be found of you,
if you will search for Me with all of your heart.
Jeremiah 29:13

Join me humbly in this search. Commit with me to hold loosely what we learn; to continually submit what we think we know back to Him so that He can remove another veil and show us more.

Roots and References

I first began to see into the family systems of my life when I received a series of audio messages by Jack Frost called "The Father Heart of God," eventually available in book form as *Spiritual Slavery to Spiritual Sonship*.[1] Like all of the truth, this was something deep in my spirit which only needed to be shaped into language. Thanks to the late Jack Frost for his articulating it, and my friend, Doug Stringer, for putting Frost's teachings in my hands. You can never know how much God can use a book, a link, a message that you pass on to someone else. I have been preaching and teaching on the topic for many years now, but much of what I share here started with Jack's teaching.

Another Jack, Pastor Jack Hayford, has had a most profound impact on my life over the past thirty-five years. Though much could be said in appreciation and fondness for a spiritual father, my aim here is to point you to a key reference. Pastor Hayford taught a series of messages to his congregation at The Church On The Way several decades ago, which served as the foundation to the book later titled *Rebuilding the Real You*.[2] It is a study of the transformational work of the Holy Spirit in each believer's life as seen through the lens of Nehemiah. Nehemiah's call to rebuild the broken-down walls of Jerusalem is a beautiful analogy of the Holy Spirit's mission to restore the broken-down walls and gates of the believer's own soul. Both of these books reveal roots of my own journey and would serve as towering companions to what I humbly offer here.

Clarifying the Terms

Two recurring terms that need clarification are *sonship* and *orphan spirit*. Due to cultural sensitivities and changes of usage, I wish to alert the reader as to how these terms are being used in this book (though it may be used in other ways elsewhere). The term *sons* does not herein denote a reference to gender, but position—a place of belonging and identity in Jesus Christ, the Son. *Sonship,* then, is about our spiritual identity and what the Scriptures declare as a believer's position in God. The Scriptures refer to believers in Jesus as "sons of God" (1 John 3:1-3). The term sons is generally used (sometimes sons and daughters), not to be sexist, but to bring out the implication of *huios*—the Greek word used for a particular kind of sonship that refers to one who has received *bar/bat mitzvah*—who is taking on partnership with the father to carry out the father's business (see Gal. 4:5-7).

Secondly, when I speak of an *orphan spirit*, I am not fundamentally referring to a spirit being, a demon spirit, or even a spiritual assignment carried out by demons, though I believe these exist. I am using the term *orphan spirit* in the way Paul uses *spirit* (Eph. 4:23), when he admonishes believers to *"be renewed in the spirit of your mind."* It could be defined as a prevailing mindset or way of thinking, a mentality or attitude. We could call it a "personal worldview," though my usage is pertaining to a sub-conscious way of thinking and seeing.

Objective

We all struggle with orphan-thinking, and the first big step is actually to see that it exists in us. Does this surprise you? There is a war raging in the world. It is not primarily a war between conservatives and progressives, capitalists and socialists, Christians and Muslims, or any skin color you might contrast. That's part of the deception. It is a war between the spirit of sonship and the orphan spirit. It is raging in every nation, every people group, outside the Church and inside the Church, on the platform and in the pew. What's the cause and what's the cost? My objective is to use numerous ways, including biblical stories, Jesus's teachings, prophetic pictures, the process leading into and out of the orphan heart, and historical examples, to articulate the contrasts between the spirit of sonship and the orphan spirit. These contrasts will give you "eyes to see"—and once you've seen it, you will not be able to "unsee" it. This is how the Holy Spirit begins to accelerate His work of transformation in you. The world is waiting for us to rise up as sons who know we are sons, and how to be sons without having to work at it.

Introduction

Is "The *Abba* Factor" about God the Father? Is it about Jesus who used the Aramaic word *Abba*? Is it about how to pray using this word? Or is it about the Holy Spirit who cries *"Abba"* in our hearts?

Yes.

It is all of that—but *The Abba Factor* is first and foremost a Trinitarian celebration of God displaying how secure He is, how He can love us unconditionally, and in His self-sufficient infiniteness be open to partnership with humanity. This is a God Who lacks nothing, needs nothing, has no holes to fill by men's praise, applause or obedience. He freely, self-assuredly loves us into the fullness of what He made us to be.

The Abba Factor is about the contrast between orphan and son, and the process of transformation from one to the other. It is about how the Holy Spirit works inside the believer's own spirit to bring him/her to a place of solid conviction and ongoing awareness of sonship—to live as a son. That sonship means there is not a place to get to—you are already there "in Christ." There is nothing you need that you don't already have "in the Spirit." It's not about what you can do, but who you "be." The striving is over. The quest for self-actualization is an illusion. "All things are yours" (John 16:15; Rom. 8:32; 1 Cor. 3:21-22; 1 John 2:20, 27). If this is true, then *being a disciple of Jesus is more about a way of being than better ways of doing*; not a quest for best practices, but freedom to be the real you. This process of transformation is bringing your mind to understand what your heart already knows. But the sooner you find out that you don't know how to do that, the better; it is the Holy Spirit within you who is doing the work.

(For the deeper focus on the nature of God as *Abba*, read *The Abba Foundation*, by Dr. Chiqui Wood, (Burkhart Books, 2018), which answers the questions as to why someone would want to have this kind of intimate relationship with God. After all, if one possesses a wrong view of God in the first place, it sabotages the desire to know God.)

The Abba Factor delves into how Holy Spirit's top priority is to process, produce, download sonship in us and how we can partner with Him to expedite that work. But first, there is an important matter of perspective.

What's the Big Deal About Using the Word Abba for God?

Let's talk about this word *"Abba."*

To distinguish what is and is not important is a major part of growing up. Good parenting is about teaching our children "values"—and values are what is important. Values cannot be assessed without perspective, so it is important that we begin with some perspective on why this idea of God, the Father of Jesus, can be called *Abba*, and just what that means. Even a brief review means that anyone who takes the message of Christ seriously looks at His (and our) Jewish roots.

To an ancient Jewish mind, it would have been irreverent, unthinkable, even blasphemous to call God by this familiar Aramaic word for *Daddy*. This is what every child in ancient Palestine would call his father in Aramaic (*Abba*, Pappa), and his mother (*Imma*, Momma). It was something new, unique and unheard of for Jesus to co-opt this common term and to speak with God as a child speaks with his father—simply, intimately, securely. It's bold, blatant and bombastic—and beyond doubt Jesus employs this term to shatter previous mindsets about God.[3] By speaking this way He reveals the very basis of His communion with God and gives us a glimpse into the life of the Trinity.

The biblical testimony is that YHWH (*Yahweh*) is used 6,519 times—more than any other personal name for God, and the most predominant metaphor is "God is King." But the least used metaphor in the Old Testament is God as father (Dt. 32:6; Is. 63:16; Jer. 3:19). God is addressed as "father" less than twenty times, and these primarily point to God as progenitor or originator (the creation came from God).[4] But Hosea provides a warm "preview of coming attractions" when he describes God's gentle, parental activity—His tender loving care for rebellious children (Israel). Hosea foresees that God is training Israel for eventual sonship, but few grasp the point that it is really about the inclusion of the nations (Hos. 11:3-4).

So, imagine the moment, what Jeremias Joachim calls "a watershed moment in human history,"[5] when the disciples (having noticed a radical difference in how Jesus talked to God), ask Jesus to teach them to pray the way He does. And without hesitation Jesus says:

> *Pray like this: "Abba in heaven ..."*
>
> Matthew 6:9

Please do not miss this.

It's not about a formulaic, right way to pray (which is exactly what we have made of it and call it "The Lord's Prayer"). It's about the moment in human history where common men are invited to know God in a way humanity had never dreamed of knowing Him—as Father to child. Those disciples were invited to move in closer, to know God intimately—not as the God who is so transcendent (and He is) and so far removed (He is not) that one dared not even pronounce His name or spell it using all the letters! In that moment Jesus was giving His disciples a look at the roadmap and mission strategy to see exactly what God was up to in sending His Son.[6] His plan was to do no less than restore fallen humanity—every nation, tribe and tongue—to a place at the Father's table where all could live as innocent, free and trusting children again.

Raymond Brown says, "Jesus's striking use of *Abba* expressed his intimate experience of God as his own father and this usage made a lasting impression on his disciples."[7]

The Fatherhood of God Revealed in the Gospels

No less than 170 times in the Gospels Jesus speaks to/of God as Father—100 times in John's Gospel alone. Jesus taught the larger circle of His disciples that God was a good father who knows what His children need (Matt. 6:32; Luke 12:30), who is merciful (Luke 6:36) with unlimited goodness (Matt. 5.45), who forgives (Mark 11:25), and desires to give the Kingdom to His children (Luke 12:32). But when Jesus has suffered, died and comes out of the tomb on the third day, He meets Mary in the garden and says"

> *Do not cling to Me, for I have not yet ascended to My Father; but go to My brethren and say to them, 'I am ascending to **My Father and your Father**, and to My God and your God.*
> John 20:17

Notice the new inclusion: My Father is your Father.

What Jesus had given as anticipation to a new kind of future in "The Lord's Prayer" is now a reality after His resurrection. The disciples did not recognize at the time that Jesus's use of *Abba* was not just His own private designation of God—it is a word which conveys revelation of who the God of Jesus is—first and foremost, The Father. But even more, it speaks of Jesus's mission and His keen awareness of that mission. As the Hebrew writer eloquently says it:

*For it was fitting for Him, for whom are all things and by whom are
all things, **in bringing many sons to glory**, to make the captain of
their salvation perfect through sufferings.*

Hebrews 2:10

Jesus's mission was not to start a new religion, to bring judgment to the
world, or to give humanity a new code of ethics. It's much larger. He came
to make sons out of orphans—to bring many sons to glory, and restore the
orphan planet to The Father of all spirits.[8]

*I shall be their father
and they my children.
They all shall be called children of the living God.*

Jubilees 1:24
(Non-Canonical Inter-Testamental source)

A New Way

Jesus's *Abba* terminology was never to be considered a unique
relationship only He could enjoy. The New Testament confirms the mission
of Jesus was to set something new in motion which would not end with
His ascension into heaven. He told His disciples that He was going away
but would send another just like Himself, the Holy Spirit, who would *"take
those things that are mine and reveal them to you"* (John 16:14). Adopted
as sons and daughters of God, empowered by the Spirit, and imitating
their elder brother, Jesus's believers could know God as *Abba*, just as Jesus
did—because the Holy Spirit is coming to establish and cultivate the same
relationship. In the infancy of the Church, Paul maintained the earthly
Jesus's own realistic practice by speaking of God as *Abba* (Rom. 8:15; Gal.
4:6), the Father (e.g., Gal. 1:1; Phil. 2:11), or Father of our Lord Jesus
Christ (e.g., Rom. 15:6; 2 Cor. 11:31).

Paul says to the believers in Rome and Galatia that it is proof of the
indwelling Holy Spirit and the ongoing process of cultivating sonship
(Rom. 8:15; Gal. 4:6). It is not about repeating this one word, *Abba*, as a
mantra, a talisman, or a code word that lets you into the secret passage way.
This is how the Holy Spirit is transforming us from glory to glory.[9] This is
where we are going in *The Abba Factor*. I hope you will keep reading.

A Realized Sonship

I have been on a journey for years learning about the spirit of sonship. This is something that is growing in me as I continue to follow hard after *Abba*. It's a work that the Lord has been doing in my own heart—through good times and bad. There are numerous leaders teaching and writing about a spirit of sonship; and we should assume this would be the case if the Holy Spirit's primary role is to convince believers of their sonship with the *Abba Cry* (Rom. 8:17; Gal. 4:1-7). It may be the single

I can say without hesitation the greatest need in the Church is for believers to experience deep transformative conviction that they are truly sons and daughters of God.

most important message for the Church in our day. After pastoring, teaching and training leaders for almost 40 years, I can say without hesitation that the greatest need in the Church is for believers to experience deep transformative conviction that they are truly sons and daughters of God. Creation is groaning in anticipation of the Church coming to an awareness of it—a realized sonship. But the broad evidence indicates the Church is still living largely from an orphan mindset.

Yes, there are two spirits (prevailing mindsets) at work in the world: an orphan spirit, and a spirit of sonship. My goal is to instill in the reader an awareness of the orphan progression and the resulting characteristics of the orphan spirit so the symptoms can be recognized. But more importantly, as Jack Frost stated decades ago, is the fact that an orphan spirit (mindset) is not cast out, taught out, counseled out, or psycho-solved; an orphan spirit is displaced by a revelation of sonship that only comes from the Father's voice into one's spirit. The Father's words always create what they speak in us. But seeing the progression of the orphan spirit only serves its highest purpose if we then identify the progression toward Sonship; that we can live in the daily confidence that He is working in us, even when we do not sense it. We can know enough from the Scriptures about how the Holy Spirit works in us through "the *Abba Cry*" that we can partner with Him in that work. Or perhaps, discovering Father's heart, we come to realize it's not so much a work as a dance.

In other words, this book (and its sequel) is not just a contrast between the two mindsets, but a how the Holy Spirit transforms us from the inside out and how we can welcome Him to accelerate that process.

He Knows How to Get Through to You

The single greatest impact on your own awareness of sonship is tied to hearing the Father's voice—the indwelling *Abba Cry* affirms you are a son. The good news is, if you have received Jesus, the Spirit of God lives in you. He is continuously speaking what Jesus has given to Him for you, and He knows how to communicate with you in a way that you will understand. He knows whether you are an auditory learner, kinesthetic learner, or a visual learner. He knows how you hear because He formed you in your mother's womb (Ps. 139:13). He knows every traumatic experience you've been through, with the resulting hurts, wounds, emotional walls, speed-bumps and hurdles. He knows your emotional triggers and the things that "turn you off." He (the indwelling Spirit) knows how to navigate all those obstacles to speak to you—to expose the lies that you have believed about yourself (and about Him)—and displace those lies with the Truth. He knows you, He knows how to get through to you, and He is speaking. In other words, you can relax. Holy Spirit has gladly taken on the responsibility of getting Father's voice through to you in a way that you can hear it.

A Tour Guide, Not a Travel Agent

I had an administrative assistant years ago (back when the position was called a secretary) who was responsible for booking my flights and itinerary for numerous international trips. She had never travelled outside of the United States, and I found myself sitting in airports for hours on end, staying in hotels when I could have been in route, and switching from planes to trains unnecessarily. I discovered the difference between someone who could make arrangements and someone who had made the trip. There is a huge difference between travel agents and tour guides (though I certainly appreciate travel agents who have made the trip).

The Holy Spirit is not just a travel agent, making arrangements and telling you where to go. He is not just giving you a map and sending you on your way. He is your tour guide. He is walking with you, in you. Yes, it is a lifelong journey, but the Lord doesn't just hand you the Bible, telling you about the great place you should go visit. He is not a travel agent that gives you some advice about where to go and helps you make the arrangements for your trip, then sends you

The single greatest impact on your own awareness of sonship is tied to hearing the Father's voice.

on your way with a "good luck—have fun!" The Lord gives you a personal tour guide, the Holy Spirit, who has already been where you need to go, and He will walk with you every step of the way. We make a grave mistake if we only consign the Holy Spirit to helping us understand the Bible. He is not just assigned to take you through **We make a grave mistake if we only consign the Holy Spirit to helping us understand the Bible.** the Bible, but to bring you as a son into the Father's bosom. He is taking you somewhere—better yet, to Someone. You can rest because it is Holy Spirit's primary focus to transform you from glory to glory (2 Cor. 3:16-18), into the image of the Son (Rom. 8:29), and He has done it a million times before.

Prayer

Would you allow me to pray for you as you open Chapter One?

Abba, we belong to You. Your tenacious, furious love is drawing us to see You for who You are. You sent Your Son to "show us the Father"— what You are really like, who You really are. Open our eyes to see You, to be over-awed by You, to see Your glory. Thank You for sending Your Spirit to confirm that we are now sons, and to convince us of the implications of that sonship. I pray that You would open our spiritual ears to hear what You are saying. Open our spiritual eyes to see what You are doing—first of all, what You are doing in us. We come in humility to say we don't see ourselves as You see us. Remove the blinders from our eyes. I ask that You reveal to this reader, this hungry soul, what it is to live with nothing to fear, nothing to prove, nothing to hide, and nothing to lose. We don't want to know about You; we want to know You.

In the name (the rule and realm) of the Father, Son, and Holy Spirit, Amen.

One

Your Invitation to "The Joy Ride"

Where else do we need to be if we be in Christ? Why the striving?
This new life is not about a place to go as much as a way to be.

I want to take you on a visual journey—a virtual tour in your imagination. It's a prophetic scene the Lord gave me to help you return to child-likeness. The first step of that "returning" is to see where you really are, and that you need to and want to make a change.

Imagine a red convertible Mustang, top down, on a journey on the open road. This car is on a highway somewhere in Southeast Colorado in early summer—driving on a highway that runs through a spacious landscape of lush, green pastureland– the mountains still snow-peaked in the distance on the right, and a crystal-clear river running with that "clear Rocky Mountain spring water" on the left. Cattle are grazing in the open pastures (they must be the happiest cows in the world), and an occasional farm house in the distance. Do you see it?

As we zoom in on the family of five in the red Mustang, it's an unsuspecting scene—at first glance nothing seems unusual. Behind the wheel, driving with a certain serene stillness is the father of the family. He is clearly enjoying this experience of taking his family on this scenic adventure. There is a slight pleasant smile—the distilling of an unconscious delight—on this father's face as he seems to be taking his family back to a childhood home or a destination he's planned for them for some time. His left elbow rests on the driver's side door and his right arm stretches straight ahead over the steering wheel, casually steering with ease. He's happy. Do you see it?

In the front passenger-side seat is his wife. Her gaze is fixed on a smart phone in her lap as she studies her Google maps app to stay aware of the exact location of the vehicle and make sure the husband doesn't take a wrong turn. Her hair is blowing in the wind as well, but it seems more of a bother—blocking her view of the small screen. The long brown hair covers her eyes again and again so that she impatiently strokes her hair behind her ears to one side and then the other. She is quietly rehearsing how far they have travelled, the miles ahead, when they will need to make the next turn, how far until the next gas station, and when the kids will be hungry. She has not glanced upward to behold the surrounding beauty for some time now, but is a conscientious navigator.

In the smallish backseat (the Mustang wasn't mom's idea) are three children ranging from eight to fifteen years of age.

Sitting behind mom is the middle-aged of the three. She is troubled about the journey. She readily admits that she "doesn't travel well." She was traumatized by an accident in her earlier years, with some recurring dreams that have kept the memory fresh in her mind. She seems to be in pain, holding her face in her hands, bending over, face down to her knees, as she rocks back and forth hoping this journey will end soon with no terrible surprises! It seems the last thing on her mind is to take in the scenery surrounding them. Perhaps, one thinks, this is why the mother is so intent upon the navigation. The father is serenely, confidently driving, the mother is intently navigating, this child seems traumatized, certainly not enjoying the ride. Do you see it?

On the left side backseat behind the father is the oldest of the three; a son sporting large "noise reduction" headphones which are attached to a PlayStation video game. He is oblivious to the surroundings and is only aware of the score he has been trying to beat for the past week. He is detached from the real world; detached from the unforgettable scenery outside the car, detached from the family inside the car, detached from reality—except for an occasional hunger pain and sensation of thirst. He can play his video games for hours uninterrupted. He also is looking down but slightly aware and annoyed that the youngest is being her usual animated self, beside him.

The youngest child is between the other two, on the bump in the smallish back seat, but not sitting down. She is standing up—precariously—hands stretched out wide, long blond curls flying in the wind—she squeals with glee. She is looking to the mountains, then to the river, then back to the pasturelands again. Over and over she shrieks, "Wow, Daddy, look at the mountains! Smell this fresh air! Have you ever seen anything like this before?" Your first thought, of course, is that standing up in the back seat of a fast-moving vehicle is dangerous. We as onlookers immediately glance back at the father expecting him to correct her and command her to "Sit down!" But instead, we see the easy smile on his face broaden into a grin. Every few seconds he is glancing in the rearview mirror to drink in her joy.

It dawns upon us as onlookers that something dynamic is going on here. He is sharing in her joy— she is manifesting his. She is the only passenger actually appreciating the glory and beauty that surrounds—the purpose for which they have made this journey. He is somehow confident that she is safe in her ecstasy. With a brilliant grin, the playful daughter glances to the rearview mirror again to see the reflection of her father's eyes—looking back through the same mirror at her own. His driving experience allows him to keep one eye on the road and the other on her. They see each other, and share the joy of creation as though they were one.

He is sharing in her joy—she is manifesting his.

Do you see it?

Does the father love this little one more than the others? Oh no. He loves his wife, of course, and all of them with all of his heart. His mind is never without the memory of the unique birth of each one. But he rejoices in the one who is rejoicing with him right now. His heart is full to know that this little one has no care, no fear, no thought of what could go wrong or when the next stop will be. She doesn't even fully realize that this—this moment—is what the trip is all about.

We will come back to this story—and the question to process in our journey together is, *where are you sitting in the red convertible Mustang?*

First Fundamental Reality of Sonship

If you've ever owned an aquarium, then you know that when you fill the tank you don't first fill it with water and then put in the big rocks. This is how the first-time aquarium owner creates a small flood in his house. No, the key is to put the big rocks in the tank first. So, let's place a big rock in the aquarium right from the start. ***God's nature is to reveal Himself—not hide Himself—from His creation***. He is a revealer, giving Himself away by His very nature, and He cannot be any other way.

The great disaster of Adam and Eve was not simply that they sinned or were disobedient to a divine rule. The disaster was that in believing the lie of the evil one, they became blind. And by "blind," I do not mean that they could not see physically. I mean that their perception of reality became skewed, so skewed that they could no longer perceive the real truth about God or about themselves.

The nature of God is to Reveal, to make Himself known. If we are designed to experience abounding life in knowing the Father's heart, in hearing His voice of affirmation and joy, and in perceiving His lavish embrace, then becoming blind to the Father is the single greatest disaster that could possibly happen to us. Adam and Eve believed a lie about God, and simultaneously believed a lie about themselves. The explicit lie about God is that He is keeping something back from His "son and daughter;" the implicit lie then is that there was something Adam and Eve did not have.

Here's how we know this.

God is not a "concealer," He is a revealer. Because He is by nature infinite, overflowing, other-centered love, totally secure in that perfect love, He has nothing to fear. He is not hiding anything from you for fear that you might do the wrong thing with that information. Just the opposite, because He is infinite love, He can't keep Himself to Himself—that is, He is infinitely outflowing—giving Himself away. He has nothing to hide, and is incapable of fear. Why? Because He is God. If He needs anything He doesn't have, He can create it. Why would He ever be afraid of losing anything?

The first lie ever perpetrated on humanity was not only that something was being kept from them, but imbedded in the lie was an inherent implication that God had a reason to hide something from them. "Those walks and talks you are having with God in the cool of the day aren't quite as transparent as you thought," Satan hints. But God wasn't hiding anything, and Adam and Eve weren't lacking anything.

This is the first big rock in the aquarium—***the nature of God is to Reveal, to make Himself known.*** God is a revealer. He has nothing to hide. He's giving Himself away completely (see Rom. 8:34), and there was nothing Adam and Eve were lacking. In having God, they had everything they would ever need. Lucifer created a doubt by depositing a thought in their minds they had never considered before. "Perhaps I don't have everything I need. Perhaps there are some things I have to do for myself. Perhaps God is just testing me to see if I have initiative." When we believe a lie about God, we believe a lie about ourselves—not because we are God (we are not), but because God made us in His image to need only Him as our source. Sons are secure in their Father's love; orphans are trying to prove they are sons.

(To become grounded in this understanding of God, see *The Abba Foundation*, by Dr. Chiqui Wood, Burkhart Books, 2018.)

The fact that God reveals Himself as a Father is one of the grandest of revelations. If you fundamentally believe God is a concealer more than a revealer, then when times get tough you will default to dismissive truisms like "God works in mysterious ways, His wonders to perform," or "You never can tell what God will do," and you will never trust that you can really know Him like a son knows a father. Nor will you believe that God really wants to know you intimately. He has not been hiding from you, but Satan lies to us about what we are seeing. Satan is happy to let you embrace a book of principles instead of a Person, disciplines of self-control over dynamic partnership. Always remember that it was God who came looking for Adam, not the other way around—and God has been seeking and revealing ever since. His first question was not, "Adam, did you break My rule?" but "Adam, where are you?" And He keeps coming, and keeps speaking (Matt. 4:4).

> *God, who at various times and in various ways spoke*
> *in time past to the fathers by the prophets,*
> *has in these last days spoken to us by His Son*
>
> Hebrews 1:1-2

Second Fundamental Reality of Sonship

The second fundamental reality is that **what you believe is the lens through which you see and interpret everything that ever happens to you.** We can actually say that whatever you believe about God will directly impact what you believe about yourself. So what you believe about yourself, will be the lens through which you see everything and interpret everything that ever happens to you, whether good or bad. Satan knows what you believe determines how you see. If you believe certain things about God, you will interpret everything that happens through the lens of that belief. This is why Satan's diabolical method is to use traumatic events that happen to a person as an entry point for a lie. He uses your traumatic experiences to lie to you about God and then about yourself. He might prompt you to say, "Where was God when I needed Him? If God really loved me He wouldn't have let that happen

Satan's diabolical method is to use traumatic events that happen to a person as an entry point for a lie.

23

The Holy Spirit will use divine encounters and transformational experiences to displace those lies with the conviction of Truth's reality.

to me. God must not love me—but I know He is a God of love, so there must be something wrong with me."

Now you might ask, "If that is the case then how can I ever change? If my interpretation of all events is preset, how do I ever break out?" The answer lies in experiences—not just head-knowledge, but God-encounters. Satan used traumatic and disappointing experiences as the Trojan horse by which he stealthily inserted his lies into your thinking. The Holy Spirit will use divine encounters and transformational experiences to displace those lies with the conviction of Truth's reality.

This may not seem like a big deal initially but think about the nature of experience. We now know that every experience we have gets hard-wired into our brains through chemicals that get released through the neurological system. A traumatic experience that causes the nervous system to go into "fight or flight" mode involves the release of adrenaline, enkephalins, endorphins, into the blood stream to enable the body to "power up" to react to an emergency. Shock is caused by such a dumping of these chemicals into the system that the brain is overwhelmed (or effectively disengaged), protecting the sensory system from too much pain or an overload of information. But these doses of adrenaline don't just disappear after the threat is over. Some of these chemicals actually bond to the neurons in the brain locking both the memory and the psychological trauma into the vault. When that memory is triggered through a similar experience or thought, the physiological response can almost be like re-living the experience again. This is why a person who has had a traumatic experience in the past will have fears, nightmares, physiological responses that seem illogical to those around them.

Experience Becomes Your Reality

My wife survived a horrific automobile accident a couple of decades ago, when she was stuck in highway traffic and rear-ended by a semi-truck travelling at 65 miles-per-hour. Though her car was smashed like an accordion, she was supernaturally spared with minimal cuts and bruises. However, to this day I have to be aware that her need for space between our car and the cars ahead or behind us is greater than mine. She sub-consciously reacts to close traffic because of the traumatic experience she lived through. Experiences, both negative and positive, get hard-wired as reality to us.

Experiences, both negative and positive, get hard-wired as reality to us.

The same is true with positive experiences. Have you ever had the experience of walking into a department store or grocery store and hearing a song playing through the speaker system that triggers a memory? Perhaps you hadn't thought of that high school flame for years, but you hear "your song" and memories come flooding in. Perhaps it's the smell of a cologne or perfume. Perhaps it's a word or phrase that has permanent memories that trigger not only a memory but an actual physiological response.

When I was in my thirties I ran in a number of 5K and 10K runs and eventually began training for a marathon. I had a certain playlist of songs I would listen to while running every day which would help keep me on pace. Most of it was my favorite jazz-fusion mix of Jeff Lorber and James Vincent. What I did not realize was that the music, continually synchronized with my running, created a physiological bond in such a way that, one day when driving from one city to another, I put my "running mix" on in the car, and the adrenaline kicked in. I didn't realize I was traveling at such a high speed until I saw the flashing red lights coming up behind me!

How do you think addictions develop? How does a guy get addicted to pornography in such a way that he just sees a girl walking down the street and suddenly something is triggered in his mind and then physical responses drive him to have to find relief for that internal "fire?" What causes a pro athlete or entertainer to keep seeking the applause and adulation of the crowds long after their skills have diminished? What causes people to maintain destructive behaviors though they know it is costing them their families, health, and eventually killing them?

This is important. God made you as a holistic being—spirit, soul and body. As much as we want to compartmentalize our physical world from our psychological and spiritual world, we are designed to be a wholeness, and these all impact each other. And Satan has watched humanity long enough to know how to play on your traumatic experiences so as to build strongholds of emotional and spiritual bondage that get triggered again and again with certain stimuli—and we keep falling into the same traps over and over and can't figure out how to get free.

Holy Spirt Re-Wires with New Experiences

If the Holy Spirit formed you in your mother's womb, don't you think He knows how to deliver you from the inter-connections between spirit, soul and body? Don't you think He knows how to replace the effects of traumatic experiences with new God-ordained experiences? Could it be that the reason Jesus said:

*The Holy Spirit who has been **with** you, will now be in you, and He will take those things of Mine and reveal them to you.*
John 14:17; 16:15

It is the indwelling Spirit that leads us into new experiences and glorious God-encounters. He actually de-programs the old triggers and replaces them with new transformative experiences that release joy, peace, and gentleness instead of fear, anger and lust.

Could it be that we cannot be transformed by information alone (good doctrine and right thinking), because the interconnectedness of our inner being requires an experience that re-wires our soul? Could this help us understand why "the Gospel is not in word only, but in power" (1 Cor. 4:20), and why Jesus told His disciples that sitting under His teaching alone wasn't enough—that they needed to go to Jerusalem and be filled with power—a new transformational experience that would begin to hard-wire them to a new reality of the Kingdom (Acts 1:8)? The more fixated the Church becomes with information, and the more She shies away from a dynamic experience, the less real transformation is seen in individuals and the less impact upon our world.

The *Abba Cry* is about how the Holy Spirit takes up His home in you, not just to teach you more information about the Bible, but to release the power of a transformative experience that re-formats your hard-drive (your spirit) and sets you free from old ways of thinking, believing and behaving.

The indwelling Spirit that leads us into new experiences and glorious God-encounters, actually de-programs the old triggers and replaces them with new transformative experiences.

(The actual science of this kind of neurological transformation is called Epigenetics, and is treated in depth in the sequel to this book entitled, *The Abba Formation*).

What Have We Said?

The first fundamental reality of sonship is to understand that God is a revealer. He has nothing to hide. He's giving Himself away completely to make Himself known.

The second fundamental reality is that what you believe is the lens through which you see and interpret everything that ever happens to you.

Whether you knew it or not, you have had an interpreter throughout your life (either Satan or Holy Spirit) interpreting every event you've ever had through the filter of your believing.

Man cannot be transformed by information alone; if information alone could transform, we would have been set free a long time ago and those with the highest IQ would naturally be the most free.

PRAYER

Abba, I may not even be aware of the traumatic experiences of my past that have opened the doors to fears, doubts, and insecurities in my life. But You know every one of them. Holy Spirit, would You bring me into Father's presence in such a way, and with such real experiences of Your Presence, that my experiences in You heal or replace the damage of the past and close the doors of my soul that have been left open from the past. I welcome You, Holy Spirit, to bring me into new things in God—exceedingly abundantly above all I could ask or think. Amen.

GROUP DISCUSSION

1. What are some examples that confirm to us that God's nature is to reveal Himself, make Himself known, rather than to conceal Himself?

2. How does Satan use traumatic experiences as entry points to build strongholds in our lives? Can you give an example?

3. What are some examples of how the Holy Spirit brings us into experiences with God that set us free from past bondages?

Two

The Orphan Spirit on an International Scale

The orphan heart is the root of every brokenness. People misunderstand the Source of their worth and thus their own worth.
—Alan Smith

The orphan spirit is not only personal but manifests globally as nation rises against nation, culture against culture. I want you to see that the ultimate diabolical intent of the orphan spirit is not only to separate you from the Father's love but to destroy humanity. The orphan spirit found its way into our planet when the first couple believed a lie about God. Suddenly there was something they didn't have that they needed to grasp (or so they thought). The fruit was just the symbol. Then there was Cain who despised his brother Abel; then Jacob who deceived Esau for the birthright and blessing; then Lot who chose the better land, and Ishmael sent away from Isaac, and one story after another throughout Scripture reveals the war had begun between something larger than race or ethnicity. The orphan spirit is out to destroy the sons of God.

We know the earth is under a curse of an orphan spirit. If you ever want to see a visual demonstration of that in a people, it was on display in 2004 in the burial procession of Chairman Yasser Arafat.[10] The world looked on as the Palestinian people demonstrated what it means not to have a home (homeland), what it is to have been refused their own property by Arab brothers.[11] They are seen as global orphans—and yet God has a destiny for them. (Paul gets to the heart of this when he contrasts Sarah and Hagar, Isaac and Ishmael, which will be examined in more detail later.) It is easy for us to sit back on our couch, watch the news, and have a nationalistic spirit arise and say, "I'm so glad I'm better than they are." But we must know that we are not any better than anybody else on this planet. All humanity is from one blood, one race of men and God has prescribed our place, our habitation for our earthly life to unfold (Acts 17:26).

The orphan mindset is on display in my own country as cultures clash and the orphan spirit wars against the spirit of sonship. There are pockets within any culture that demonstrate deeply ingrained beliefs (spiritual and psychological defaults) that pit the "haves and have-nots" against one another based on the lie that "someone is keeping something from you" (the lie of the Garden). Sociologists are still studying the 1968 L.A. riots in Watts to understand why one minority lashed out against another minority. Why did it seem that immigrant cultures coming into the U.S. were gaining ground and building wealth faster than other cultures that seemed to be forever stuck in poverty and despair? How have the Jewish people historically been able to not only survive but thrive in every culture they have been scattered into over the centuries? How have the Asian cultures come more recently into North America, and within a short period of time owned their own shops, businesses, and corporations? Is there a mindset, a preset or default that makes the difference? Do cultures that embrace a relational, familial worldview (with a sense of father, home, and inheritance) fare better than those that celebrate an individualistic worldview? And what's the difference between shame-based cultures and guilt-based cultures?

The point is that the orphan spirit may have slightly different symptoms in different cultures, and it may have slightly different symptoms from one generation to the next, but it's universal to the human family.

Famous People with Bad Father Relationships

We can shift the lens from the macrocosm of cultures to the microcosm of families and individuals. There is no shortage of tragic stories of famous people, successful people, high-achieving people, whose lives ended in the despair of endless pursuits of passions, possessions, positions or power. One only need google "famous people with bad endings" or "famous people, bad parents," or anything similar, to see the tragic and repetitive stream.

Would it be a surprise to discover a connection between atheism and damaged father relationships? In the autobiographical movie, *A Case for Christ*, the atheist and award-winning Boston Globe journalist, Lee Strobel, set out to disprove the resurrection of Christ. He was struck by the hard evidence that over 500 eyewitnesses had seen Jesus post-resurrection, so he sought out a leading psychologist concerning the possibility of mass hallucinations. Roberta Waters, President of the American Association of Psychoanalysts and leading authority on Human Behavior at Purdue University (at that time), noticed something about Strobel's personal angst that was driving his pursuit. The agnostic psychologist said, "I imagine as a skeptic you're familiar with history's great names in atheism: Hume, Nietzsche, Sartre, Freud …"

"Yes, of course," Strobel responded, "some of my greatest heroes."

Dr. Waters continued, "Did you know that all of them had a father who either died when they were young, abandoned them, or was physically or emotionally abusive? In the world of therapy, it's called a father-wound."[12]

Strobel, recounting the conversation later, says,

> I was oblivious to the fact that a young person's relationship with his father can greatly color his attitude toward God. I wasn't aware that many well-known atheists through history including Friedrich Nietzsche, David Hume, Bertrand Russell, Jean-Paul Sartre, Albert Camus, Arthur Schopenhauer … Voltaire, HG Wells, Madalyn Murray O'Hair, and others had felt abandoned or deeply disappointed with their fathers, making it less likely they would want to know a heavenly father.[13]

The orphan spirit has been so abundantly documented in newspapers, news channels, and history that there is no point to produce a litany of stories here. The fact is, we almost expect people "out there" to lose their moral compass and self-destruct somewhere along the way. It is a sadistic orphan sport to build a new superstar up to the point they cannot possibly sustain their own fame and wealth, just so society can watch them come crashing down (perhaps with some private glee that we haven't messed up that badly ourselves).

We don't expect the orphan spirit to show up in the powerful, achiever side of society. But the *Abba* Factor reveals that sonship is not about wealth, education, entitlement or privilege (or the lack thereof). Quite the opposite, we find the orphan spirit equally at work in every stratum of society, among the educated and illiterate alike, every community and geography. It may look more sophisticated in some places than others, more "successful" in some stories than others, but one is either an orphan or a son.

A Strong Family-Life is No Guarantee

The orphan spirit gains inroads in our lives with the temptation to focus on the faults that we see in parental (and eventually governmental) authority at various levels. We all have stories about our parents' imperfections. In the more healthy families, you can sit around the table at Thanksgiving

Satan uses the imperfections of those that God has put in authority in our lives as entry points for an orphan spirit. and Christmas and laugh about them. You can laugh about things Dad used to do when you were growing up, or the things Mom used to say. In the healthier families, there is some dialogue about our common frailty. But there has never been a perfect parent; there's never been a perfect pastor; there's never been a perfect president, or governor, or teacher. And so it is that Satan uses the imperfections of those that God has put in authority in our lives as entry points for an orphan spirit.

I have been one of those homeschool dads who blew the trumpet for a return to a strong home and family life. I have sought to highlight the differences between Western world individualism and the Hebraic ethos of shared life. I can argue the negative effects of individualistic and dualistic philosophies, the negative impacts of the early-American Industrial revolution upon the home, and the need to return to a family culture. But the problem is deeper than a lack of "quality family time."

Scripture is filled with transparent stories of good fathers and bad ones. One of the qualities we must cherish from the Scriptures is the refusal only to show the good side of the story. God's revelation to us is transparent, authentic and unvarnished. This includes some blatant failures in the vocation of fatherhood. In the Scriptures, we can turn through the photo album of history to observe fathers who demonstrate both wisdom and foolishness—fathering from an orphan heart or a spirit of sonship.

ADAM—As the first man and first human father, he had no example to follow except God. He faltered on that, plunging the world into sin. He also had to deal with the tragedy of his son Cain murdering his brother Abel. Have you ever wondered what impact Abel's murder had on Adam? Did he blame himself? In what way did his own attempts to perform and make up for his failure in the Garden impact Cain's idea of strength and acceptance? How does the orphan spirit reveal itself in Adam?

NOAH—Noah stands out as a father in the Bible who clung to God in spite of the wickedness all around him. It is also apparent that his own children honored and revered him, serving him for 100 years to complete a fantastic mission. What could be more relevant today? He bravely carried out the task God assigned to him, and yet we see that he wasn't perfect. What can we learn about parenting, or the implications of the *Abba* Factor—as to why Ham would respond one way to Noah's failure, and Shem and Japheth respond another (Gen. 9:21-23)?

ABRAHAM, "father of nations"—What could be more frightening than to carry the promise of nations within you? That was the mission God gave Abraham. He was a leader with tremendous faith, passing one of the most difficult tests God ever gave a man. Even after numerous altar experiences of commitment, worship and thanksgiving, we are allowed to see Abraham make mistakes when he attempts to control the situation. In what way do we see both the strengths and weakness being passed on to his children (e.g., his lying about Sarah being his sister instead of his wife [Gen. 20:1-18] is repeated by his son and grandson)? And how were these strengths and weaknesses passed on? Genetically? Through divine attribution? By bitterness and resentment? We don't tend to think of Father Abraham as having anything of orphan heart; but why would he lie about his wife to save his own skin? Is it something else?

ISAAC, son of Abraham—Many fathers feel intimidated trying to follow in the footsteps of their own father, especially the footsteps of greatness. Isaac must have felt this burden. His father Abraham grew to be such a wealthy and powerful patriarch. Was Isaac mindful of the burden or did it seem natural to him? Did he wrestle with bitterness and resentment because his father was willing to offer him as a sacrifice? Yet we see Isaac as an obedient son, with a strong attachment to his mother (Gen. 24:67). Why did Isaac also have a weakness for lying about his wife (Gen. 26:7)?

JACOB—He was a schemer who tried to work his own way instead of trusting God. With the help of his mother Rebekah, he stole his twin brother Esau's birthright. Jacob fathered 12 sons who founded the 12 tribes of Israel. As a father, however, he favored his son, Joseph, causing jealousy among the other brothers. What do we learn from Jacob's life about gaining a new identity by his wrestling with God? Do we ever see Jacob revert back to his old identity? In what way do we have "power with God" as sons?

MOSES, giver of the Law—Moses was the father of two sons, Gershom and Eliezer, yet he was known as the father of the entire Hebrew people as they escaped from slavery in Egypt. He patiently loved them and helped discipline and provide for them on their 40-year journey to the Promised Land, but not without his own impatience. How can the "meekest man in all the earth" rashly murder an Egyptian taskmaster, hurl the stone tablets down the mountain (autographed by God, no less), and strike the rock twice? What does Moses reveal (albeit an Old Testament figure who is not filled with the Spirit as we would understand it in the New Testament) about our human frailty, even in the meekest of men? What do we do with such cautions? Is it possible to be a godly man and still deal with orphan issues?

KING DAVID—Noted as a man after God's own heart, David is one of the great paradoxes in the Bible. David trusted God to help him defeat the lion, the bear, and Goliath. He kept his faith anchored in God though he was on the run from King Saul for almost twenty years. David was a miserable model of a father during his early years. He sinned greatly, but wept bitterly, repented deeply, and found forgiveness. His son Solomon was the beneficiary of David's personal revival and went on to be regarded as Israel's greatest king.

KING SOLOMON—the wisest man in all the earth, is an interesting study in starting well and finishing poorly. God granted him not only his request for wisdom but long life and prosperity. But he took 3,000 wives, many from foreign lands, and eventually penned Ecclesiastes as the antithesis to Proverbs. Proverbs speaks of certainty in the ways of God— Ecclesiastes testifies to no certainty at all. It is as though Solomon lived to fulfill his father's unfinished business (building the Temple), then lost his way in an abundance of exploits that did not satisfy. What can we learn from Solomon about the Father's mission and the son's obedience?

When we think of great men of God in our world today, is there one who is exempt from the struggle between sonship and the orphan spirit? Does this mean that there is no real transformation, that transformation is just religious terminology, or is it a lifelong process?

The Orphan Spirit Is Also No Respecter of Persons

Doug Wead has researched the lives and families of all the American Presidents and many other national leaders seeking to find a link between the father's influence and the child that eventually became an American President. At the time of the 2008 U.S. presidential campaign, the last two opponents standing were both men who had barely known their fathers: Barack Obama and John McCain. Presidents Andrew Jackson and Bill Clinton never knew their fathers; these men had died before the sons were born.

The father of Barack Obama left home in 1963 when his son was only two years old. They were separated by continents. Obama was twenty-one years old when he learned by a telephone message that the father he never knew was killed in an automobile accident. History now records Obama serving two consecutive terms as President of the United States. John McCain, historically the only son and grandson of four-star Admirals in the Navy, had a father who was very loving but very busy and mostly absent. In fact, history shows that many fathers of the American presidents died young. And even the ones who lived longer were busy, successful, but absent. George Herbert Walker Bush said of George W., "I was never there. Barbara raised him." That said, he was one of only two fathers actually to attend their sons' inaugurations.

What impact would that have had on young men seeking to prove or measure up? The truth is, Hitler, Stalin, Chairman Mao all fit the pattern of a strong mother attachment and an absent father. What is baffling, outside of an understanding of the orphan spirit, is that it seems to be the template for aggressive and criminal behavior as well as that of highest performers.

America's prisons are full of young men who love their mothers and don't know their fathers. Wead concludes, "It seems that both presidents and criminals drink from the same poison cup with vastly differing results. It was a strange tonic for good to the achieving presidents and a formula for terrible emotional damage to the criminal."[14]

Here is the point: authority figures are not perfect—whether parents, pastors, teachers, or politicians—and Satan uses their imperfections as entry points for an orphan spirit into sons and daughters.

How Did This Happen to Me?

Adam and Eve believed that God was keeping something from them but letting on that they only needed Him. They saw it as a flaw in God. They are not the only humans who believe they have seen a flaw in God. They are not the only ones who have been mad at God. But the cause for most is so subtle that we find ourselves asking, "How did this happen to me?"

Absalom had watched his pre-occupied King-of-a-father fail to deal with the pressing family issues. He was busy building Israel into the greatest nation on earth. But at the palace, having blindly given consent to Amnon to be alone with his half-sister, who then took the opportunity

Absalom's rise to the throne is a picture of an orphan grasping for what the son had received by gift and there are many orphans sitting in high places. to rape her, David did nothing. He covered the family shame by isolating Tamar permanently in the palace. The other sons seethed, took up an offense for Tamar, and fell in with Absalom to kill Amnon. This was the orphan seed planted in Absalom that led to an eventual coup against his own father. He would sit at the city gate, hear the complaints of the people about this father, and agree with them. "I could rule better ... you see, I am here listening to your trouble ... King David is too busy up in his palace." Absalom's rise to the throne is a picture of an orphan grasping for what the son had received by gift. And there are many orphans sitting in high places—but they are driven, grasping, forced to multiply the deceptions to stay in power.

Some time ago I was speaking to the congregation I served about the Father's love, and I said something from the pulpit that wounded one of my own children. I told a family story that embarrassed my daughter—she felt it revealed a weakness in her—and I had not received permission to tell it. It was my mistake, and it was received as rejection. I certainly didn't intend it as such, but in my thoughtlessness, even attempting to preach about the Father's love, I wounded my daughter and had to seek her forgiveness.

How much we would give to have all those mistakes back—but we have to seek forgiveness and keep coming to the Father for fresh fullness to overflow His love in us, and then through us to others. The fact remains, every one of us has the opportunity to either focus on the failures of those that God has put in our lives or to forgive. That focus turns to receiving their faults as either discouragement, a rejection of self, or an opportunity to grow in God. Discouragement is the emotional response to a failed expectation.

We can't help but have expectations. Expectations are a result of learning, and learning is most fundamentally our brain's ability to log and categorize previous events. The brain stores memories in the neatest patterns possible to minimize having to process every bit of incoming data again and again, as if every experience was a first. This is why you can **Discouragement is the emotional response to a failed expectation.** get in your car in the morning, drive to work, travel the same route as before without having to look at a map, and then later never really remember the drive. Your brain didn't process much of the data as unique, so there are few vivid memories.

But as children, much of what is happening is new. We are especially watching how our parents act, think and speak because they are our primary source of provision, safety, and well-being. We are learning from every new thing that is happening, and we are building expectations. Can you see how we would put so many expectations upon our parents, and how important those would be for us? We want to believe them, so we learn to pressure our parents to make promises, thinking that if they promise, in their goodness they will have to keep it. Sometimes even good parents forget, or something comes up that disrupts a plan. But when the promise is broken, it opens the door to other things. None of us have had perfect parents, our little hearts get hurt, we get disappointed, and the enemy misinterprets our reality to us to worm his way in. And thus, it begins.

But there is a standing invitation—a way to the Father, and a revelation of the Father that carries with it a mutual revelation of sonship. In the next chapter, we consider how Jesus came to extend an invitation to sonship and show us the way to the Father. But right now, is there a wound from your father or mother that has become an inroad for the enemy to build lies, resentments, or strongholds? Do you need to have a conversation with your Heavenly Father before we move forward?

What Have We Said?

The orphan spirit is visible on a global scale; all of the conflict of the Middle East can be understood as an ongoing war between sons and orphans—those that have a homeland and those who do not.

We can see that the orphan spirit is not just about what bad people do, but is at work in all of us, even the great patriarchs of the Scripture.

People in both high and low places are driven by an orphan mindset.

Satan uses the imperfections of those that God has put in authority in our lives as entry points for an orphan spirit. And none of us get perfect parents.

Prayer

Abba, I see that everyone, from Presidents to the poorest of the poor can struggle with the orphan spirit—some with good parents and some

without—under a bondage of fear to prove, to hide, to compensate, cling to something other than You. Would You open the eyes of my heart and let me see where I am not seeing myself as You see me? Would You come to me? Break the fear of not doing enough or being enough. I open my heart and trust you with it.
In Him, Amen.

GROUP DISCUSSION

1. What are some examples of "great men" of the Bible who had signs of an orphan spirit?

2. Who are some U.S. Presidents that excelled in their fields, driven to prove something?

3. Where do we see the imperfections of one generation being passed down to the next?

Three

The Father's Invitation to Sonship

This resurrection life you received from God is not a timid,
grave-tending life. It's adventurously expectant, greeting God with
a childlike "What's next, Papa?" God's Spirit touches our spirits
and confirms who we really are. We know who He is,
and we know who we are: Father and children.

Romans 8:15 (The Message)

There is a standing invitation for humanity to enjoy the glory of sonship. Man is beckoned to understand what it means to belong and what it means to have a home. Creation shouts the truth that there is nothing one can do to deserve that glory, except to know that we have a Father who loves us and accepts us as we are. Sonship is a place in the Father's bosom.

The glory (manifest presence) of God is not something that we earn our way into (not even by repenting enough, humbling ourselves enough, or fasting long enough to earn it somehow)—though there is a place for such spiritual hunger. The glory of God is the home of Presence where the sons and daughters of God live. And the primary hindrance to living in that glory is the orphan spirit. We will either believe the voice of the Father of heaven that says, "You are My son, you are My daughter." Or we will believe the father of lies that says, "Has God said …? Could that really be true? Do you really belong to Him? Are you really His? If you really are a son of God, you would not act like this or He would not have let such and such happen."

Two Spirits in the World: Orphan Spirit vs. Sonship

Let's be brave enough to pull the mask off this thing and bring it into the light.

There are two spirits that are at war in the world today. One is a spirit of sonship, and the other is an orphan spirit. Human clutching, grabbing, scratching, achieving, and the ladder-climbing is driven by an orphan spirit.

There are two spirits that are at war in the world today; a spirit of sonship, and an orphan spirit.

You see, that spirit leads you to believe that you don't deserve anything. Then that same orphan spirit will cause you to say, "Everybody owes me something." The orphan spirit will always make you feel out of place and will lead you to believe the lies of *the father of lies*. You'll believe that somehow you don't deserve it, you're not worthy of it, or you don't fit. So, you have to grasp for everything you can get, and life becomes a competition of acquiring position, power, and possessions.

My mention of a movie is not to be misunderstood as a recommendation; but in the Christmas movie "Elf" with Will Ferrell, the lead character is an orphaned child who ends up living with Santa in the North Pole. The problem is that he's 6'4" in a world with small elf people. Nothing fits right. The toilets, the showers, nothing is his size. He always feels out of place. He even comments, "It seems like everyone has the same talents except me." It is a picture of what we all believe. Everyone else gets it but not me. There's just something off, and I can't quite put my finger on it. Until one day he finds out that his real dad is somewhere else.[15]

The spirit of sonship, on the other hand, is a spirit of belonging, a spirit of being at home, a spirit of the heir and the inheritance. *When you live from a spirit of sonship, the restless chase is over.* A spirit of sonship says, "I don't have to grasp for something that's already mine." When you have a spirit of sonship, you understand there is a place at the table with your name on it, and the plate is fully loaded, and there's more where that came from. When you have a spirit of sonship, it is understood that it's not what you do, but who you are that matters. And in this sense, it is true that what matters is not what you know but Who you know. We see how Jesus, knowing He was a Son dwelling in the bosom of the Father, was truly free. Paul says in Philippians 2:6, that Jesus "did not think that being equal with God was something to be grasped." He didn't have to grasp for equality with God because He knew He already had it—He was in the Father, and the Father was in Him (John 14:11; 17:21). This is the freedom of sons. It's the conscious conviction of current reality, the awareness of sonship.

The characteristics of sonship in their simplest form are: Sons know who their father is, thus they know they have a home, they know they belong, and they know they have an inheritance. Therefore, they don't have to grasp for something that is not theirs. When your

> **Sons know who their father is, thus they know they have a home, they know they belong, and they know they have an inheritance.**

father is God, everything is yours (1 Cor. 3:21, 22; Rom. 8:32). We will take this up in detail in Chapters 9 through 11.

On the other hand, the characteristics of an orphan spirit in their simplest form are these: the orphan doesn't know who his father is (or he believes his father has abandoned him), thus he doesn't feel he has a home, does not know where he belongs, and doesn't know if he has an inheritance. The result is that the orphan spirit spends unimaginable energy trying to acquire position, possessions, anything that will validate his worth. Taking from that which belongs to sons is especially attractive.

> **The result is that the orphan spirit spends unimaginable energy trying to acquire position, possessions, anything that will validate his worth.**

The Greatest Freedom

Pete Cantrell says, "The greatest freedom is having nothing to prove."[16] When you know who you are, you don't spend your energy trying to prove who you are. You can rest. Jesus invited us to enter into His rest (Matt. 11:28-29). Do you think He was talking about getting to heaven someday and cooling our feet in the river that flows from the throne? Or do you think He was saying, "If you come to know who you are in Me (as sons in the Son) you will have nothing left to prove." Jesus did not consider being equal with God a thing to be grasped (because it was already who He was), so He could relax and give Himself away to others.

Moses often demonstrated a sense of sonship as a result of being in God's presence. Even when the sons of Korah and others would come to try to pull him out of his place, rather than trying to defend himself, he would simply fall on his face and ask God to show them who had called him.

Two "spirits" (mindsets) are vying for humanity; the spirit of sonship is at war against an orphan spirit. To set the stage, I want you to hear this with the understanding that we're all somebody's child. All of us are children in the sense that we were there once, and in a spiritually redemptive sense, our

> **The *Abba Cry* is about the Father's tenacious work by the Spirit through the Son, to restore us to full trust in the Father's love, and ultimately to the pristine image of God as the image-bearers we were created to be.**

Our orphan nature promotes a tendency within us to focus on the negatives, the faults and failures of our flawed natural parents.

heavenly Father wants to take us back to that place of child-likeness again. The *Abba Cry* is about the Father's tenacious work by the Spirit through the Son, to restore us to complete trust in the Father's love and ultimately to the pristine image of God as the image-bearers we were created to be.

Every one of us was born with an orphan spirit. It is very strange that one would be born into a home of loving parents, and into a family—hopefully, most of us have that heritage—but at the same time born under an orphan spirit. From the day Adam and Eve were banished from the garden, an orphan spirit has been upon the human race. Banished from Father's house, the children of humanity have been under the orphan curse.

Now, we have an opportunity to learn what love is by a father and a mother, by natural parentage. God's design from the beginning is to set us in a loving family to shape our view of God as provider, caregiver, mercy-shower, and gift-developer. But our orphan nature promotes a tendency within us to focus on the negatives, the faults, and failures of our flawed natural parents. And if we focus on the failures of those that God has given us to submit to, it becomes very difficult for us to break out of that orphan thinking and to hear Father's voice.

Young people will receive daily doses of parental instruction; some out of a motivation of love, and frankly, some out of a sheer desire for obedience and compliance. But whatever the motivation, you will have the opportunity to learn from what they do right, as well as from what they do wrong.

My father often told me, "Kerry, when you grow up you will have kids, and when you do you're going to either parent them the same way I parented you, or you're going to parent them just the opposite." I have found that to be true, and the difference depends upon how I receive my parents' love, either by focusing on their expressed love or by focusing on their flaws and failures.

Jesus came to the earth declaring a spirit of sonship is available for all. He breaks the mold. He's the first among all the voices of the prophets and all who had declared the Word of God, to reveal God in the context of sonship. Until now God had been Almighty, Creator, Law-giver, and Enforcer. Now Jesus is using totally different language to talk about God. He calls Him Father. When we read the words that He spoke in the four

Gospels, Jesus is always talking in the context of Father and Son. He says He came from the Father's bosom; He only does that which pleases the Father; He only says what He hears the Father saying, and does what He sees the Father doing, and His Father delights in Him, and He delights in the Father. He and His Father are one, and one day He will go back to be with the Father. Everything Jesus talks about springs from of a spirit of sonship, and He is revealing to an orphan world what it is to have the love of the Father.

The Orphan Lie

If Christians are more tuned in to the world than to the voice of the Heavenly Father, could Christian thinking, in general, be more aligned with the father of lies? It's a rhetorical question, but the point is, unless we are radically tuned to Father's voice we think as orphans. And religion is not exempt. We don't understand our position as sons. Every religion will ensnare us with the belief that we have to do something else to get what God has for us. But Father has sent His Spirit into our hearts. Are we listening?

Orphans Grasp for Sons' Inheritance

It is important to realize that the father of the orphan spirit is Satan himself. When he was cast out of heaven, he became the first orphan; the first *without a father, without an inheritance, without a home*. Lies and manipulation are the language of that spirit, and Lucifer convinced one-third of the angels to follow him. When the father of orphans was cast into the earth, he immediately began to lie to the son and daughter, who were the vice-regents of the planet. They were used to walking in the cool of the day with the Father and enjoying His fellowship and all His provision. They needed nothing. But the chief orphan lied to the son and said, "You don't really have everything you need. God is keeping something from you. Has God said …? Don't you know that if you just eat from that tree, you'll be just like Him?" This is exactly what Lucifer had believed on the very mountain of God. It is the picture of the orphan grasping for the son's inheritance. And Man (Adam and Eve) believed the lie, and they were banished from Father's house—not because Father loved them any less, but because their spirit had been reborn in reverse: from life to death.

God delivered His people out of slavery. The people of God, had lived as orphans for 430 years; ten generations in slavery will produce a slave mentality.

Then that orphan spirit, on the back of the nature of sin and death, began to find its way from generation to generation. The orphan spirit came upon Cain and slew his brother, who was accepted. The orphan spirit came upon Esau, and the orphan spirit came upon Ishmael, who was cast out of the house. And when you watch the evening news, you see the orphan spirit grasping for the inheritance of the son. The orphan is trying to get the land that has been declared by Father as belonging to the son. The orphan spirit tries to crush the son, pull down the son, usurp his place. Please don't hear a political statement in what I just said. The good news is that every orphan can be a son. The Spirit of Adoption has been sent out into the world. He loves all peoples as much as He loves any son. But any culture that assumes an inherent right to take what is another's is blinded by an orphan spirit.

God delivered His people out of slavery. The people of God had lived as orphans for 430 years; ten generations in slavery will produce a slave mentality. So, when God brings them out by His mighty power, they spend forty years wandering in the desert until the orphan thinking is driven out of them. It's called bondage through unbelief. And those that survive and learn a new way of thinking finally get in the Promised Land.

A Sonship Training Manual

During those forty years, God gave Moses the first five books of the Bible—the Pentateuch—in order to retrain the people of God from an orphan mentality to a son mentality; from a slave mindset to a warrior-conqueror mindset. And He said, "When you come into the Promised Land I'm going to give you houses you didn't build, wells you didn't dig, vineyards you didn't plant. There's going to be iron and copper and ore in those mountains, and everything you need will be there" (Deut. 8). That's the message of a Father to a son:

"You'll never lack for anything. There will be milk and honey. The grapes will be huge. Everything you need will be there. But remember this: there's going to be an orphan spirit in that land, and you're going to have to overcome it. You will face giants that tell you it isn't yours and you don't belong, and you'll have to pull them down one by one. Don't forget who your Father is. But you will have what you need to have when you need to have it because I've already put it there for you."

There are giants in the land, and those giants have an orphan mentality. If you think you can't defeat them, it reveals the mindset that prevails in you.

So, God used Moses to retrain the people of Israel from an orphan spirit to a conquering spirit—the spirit of sonship, mastery, and authority. The New Testament believer who walks in an awareness of sonship is not a bragging, arrogant person saying, "I am somebody, and you are not, get out of my way!" Rather, a New Testament son carries a sense of peace and dignity, knowing where they came from and that they didn't earn anything they possess. In Jesus, you know who you are, and you know where you're going, so you can relax. You can say, "I don't have to prove to anybody who I am. I don't have to be super-spiritual, show off my super-gifts, prove anything by the things I possess. In fact, these aren't for me anyway—I have freely received to give freely."

Sonship Includes Humility

Just because you are a believer in Jesus does not mean that you are free from an orphan mentality. Reading the letter written to the Hebrew Christians, *The Epistle to the Hebrews*, you will find these believers are being pulled by this orphan spirit to think they have to return to Torah observance—to keep the Law of Moses to be accepted. So the writer to the Hebrews spends the first three chapters establishing that God has not just given us Moses, or the angels, or the Law, but He's given us His Son. He wants to bring many sons to glory (Heb. 2:12), so He sends us a Son to take us there. His Son is better than Moses, better than angels, better than the Law; and His Son gives us entrance into sonship by a better covenant based upon better promises (Heb. 8:6).

Evidently, those Christians, Messianic Jews, and proselytes living in Jerusalem and Judea at the time were dealing with an orphan spirit that says, "OK, you can believe in Jesus, but you still have to do all the ceremonial law. There's something yet to be grasped. Jesus, plus the Law. And if you don't keep the Law you better be afraid."

Just because you are a believer in Jesus does not mean that you are free from an orphan mentality.

45

It's the "bondage again to fear." The Hebrew writer goes on to declare the principle of faith (as established by Abraham, not Moses) and, in essence, says, "If you require anything in addition to Jesus to be righteous, that's coming from the orphan lie of religion."

Please remember that when God gave us Jesus, He freely gave us everything (Rom.8:32), which means you don't need to add anything to it for your salvation.

Prodigals, Orphans or Fathers?

In Luke chapter 15 we find Jesus's famous story of the prodigal son (actually a story about the nature and heart of the *Abba* of Jesus). This is a story about two sons and their father. Most of us know the story well. But here is an important question: which of the two sons has an orphan spirit?

I know you are very familiar with the story, but I want you to see what Jesus was trying to show us about the Father.

> *Then He said: "A certain man had two sons. And the younger of them said to his father, 'Father, give me the portion of goods that falls to me.' So he divided to them his livelihood. And not many days after, the younger son gathered all together, journeyed to a far country, and there wasted his possessions with prodigal living.*
> *But when he had spent all, there arose a severe famine in that land, and he began to be in want. Then he went and joined himself to a citizen of that country, and he sent him into his fields to feed swine. And he would gladly have filled his stomach with the pods that the swine ate, and no one gave him anything.*
> Luke 15:11-16

So far in the story, who is giving him something? The father. The father willingly divided the inheritance. Now he's out of sight of father's house and, what is he getting? Nothing.

Which of the two sons has an orphan spirit? *But when he came to himself, he said, 'How many of my father's hired servants have bread enough and to spare, and I perish with hunger! I will arise and go to my father and will say to him,*

"Father, I have sinned against heaven and before you,
and I am no longer worthy to be called your son.
Make me like one of your hired servants."

Luke 15:17-19

This is orphan thinking.

And he arose and came to his father. But when he was still a great
way off, his father saw him and had compassion,
and ran and fell on his neck and kissed him. And the son said to him,
"Father, I have sinned against heaven and in your sight,
and am no longer worthy to be called your son."

Luke 15:20-21

Before he could articulate his well-prepared orphan script ("I'll just sleep in the farmhouse with the hired servants …"), the father interrupted him.

But the father said to his servants, "Bring out the best robe and put it
on him and put a ring on his hand and sandals on his feet.
And bring the fatted calf here and kill it, and let us eat
and be merry; for this, my son was dead and is alive again; he was
lost and is found." And they began to be merry.

Luke 15:22-23

Let me ask you about this father that Jesus is talking about. Is he more interested here in compliance and obedience, or in relationship? This orphan-minded son doesn't know his father. He knows that he squandered half of his father's living, so he assumes that if he approaches him like a servant, that father will be OK because servants obey and comply. So orphan thinking says, "If I just comply and obey, Father will be happy." But he gets a new revelation of his father's heart. His father is not just interested in compliance and obedience, but he says, "We're going to have a party."

Now the story shifts to the other son:

Now his older son was in the field.

Luke 15:25

47

This son was dutiful; faithful.

> *And as he came and drew near to the house, he heard music*
> *and dancing. So he called one of the servants and asked what these*
> *things meant. And he said to him, "Your brother has come, and*
> *because he has received him safe and sound,*
> *your father has killed the fatted calf."*
> *But he was angry and would not go in. Therefore his father came out*
> *and pleaded with him. So he answered and said to his father,*
> *"Lo, these many years I have been serving you; I never transgressed*
> *your commandment at any time; and yet you never gave me a young*
> *goat, that I might make merry with my friends.*
> *But as soon as this son of yours came, who has devoured your*
> *livelihood with harlots, you killed the fatted calf for him."*
> Luke 15:25-30

If I were to ask, "Which of these two sons has an orphan spirit?", most assume it is the prodigal son that squandered his inheritance.

Both of them are bound up in orphan thinking. One of them is outside the house, living like an orphan. The other is living inside the father's house, working diligently in the fields, but thinking like an orphan. He looks at the fact that he is serving the father; that he is faithful and duty-bound. He is obedient and compliant and angry! That's the picture of much of the Church: duty-bound, faithful, serving, showing up on time, teaching the class and angry because there are others who just came off the street—drug-addicts; messed up, but got saved—and they're happy! Every prayer that they throw up to heaven gets answered! So we say, "God, I've been teaching Bible classes to these fifth-grade boys for twenty years, but my prayers aren't getting answered! That's unfair."

And Father answers:

> *"Son, you are always with me, **and all that I have is yours.***
> *It was right that we should make merry and be glad, for your brother*
> *was dead and is alive again, and was lost and is found."*
> Luke 15:31-32

If the devil cannot keep you out of Father's house, he will keep you bound up in orphan thinking inside Father's house. He'll keep you thinking that if you're just obedient and compliant, and if you work hard enough, do all the right things, give in the offerings, that somehow that will buy the Father's pleasure. Jesus, plus something else. But you need to know that *your Father is not as interested in your obedience and compliance as He is in your intimacy*.

If the devil cannot keep you out of Father's house, he will keep you bound up in orphan thinking inside Father's house.

What He wants is for you to be free to dance at the Father's party of divine life. He wants you to know that you can come boldly any time and say, "Daddy, here I am."

Do you remember the red Mustang convertible (see Chapter One)? Which seat would you say the prodigal son is in? Which seat would the elder brother be sitting in? Which seat are you in?

What Have We Said?

God sent a personal invitation to the orphan world by sending His own Son, to show us what the Father is really like, and to know a way has been prepared to Father's house.

Sons know who their father is, they know they have a home and know they have an inheritance.

Our orphan nature promotes a tendency within us to focus on the negatives, the faults, and failures of our flawed natural parents and leaders.

Even the First Century Jewish believers in Messiah had struggled with an orphan spirit and were tempted to go back to the Law of Moses: Jesus plus something else.

In Jesus's story of The Father's Heart (we call it The Prodigal Son story), we discover that one son was defiant, and the other compliant, but both lived as orphans rather than enjoying intimacy with the father.

Prayer

Father, I know You are a good God, and I know that every good and perfect gift comes from You. But if there is any place where I have accused you of doing things that You did not do, would You forgive me? I see through Jesus that You are my Father, You give me a "home" and an inheritance (Rom. 8:16-17). You have made me a joint-heir with Jesus Christ. All I need or ever will need, You have already made available through Christ. Would you continue to speak to me about what this means and how I can walk in this inheritance? Amen.

GROUP DISCUSSION

1. What are the "two spirits" (mindsets) that are at war in the world today?

2. What are the three primary things a son knows about himself according to Romans 8:14-17?

3. In the "Prodigal Son Story" which of the two sons were motivated by an orphan spirit?

Four

The Fathering Spirit Has Come

*You will either live your life as if you have a home
or as if you don't have a home.*
—Henri Nouwen

The old German proverb says, "The main thing is that the main thing remains the main thing." The tragedy of the orphan spirit is that it places a filter over the soul that causes one to misinterpret every situation, always replacing the main thing (relationship with the Father, through the Son, by the Spirit) with secondary things that never satisfy.

Have you ever been on a tour to Israel? When I first went to Israel in my twenties, I had idealized notions of the holy sites I would see. I had grown up reading the Scriptures and had these scenes created in my imagination. I was sorely disappointed to discover that every significant holy site has a cathedral built right on top of it: the Mount of Transfiguration, the Garden Tomb, the birthplace of Jesus, etc. A huge cathedral sits on top of each site. The "main thing" was submerged under secondary things. And likewise, we have made relationship with the Father a secondary thing to all the things that Christianity promotes. Through the lens of the orphan spirit, often with the best of intentions, we've taken the Father's promises of relationship and divine partnership and applied them to our orphan life as things to be grasped. This was the challenge in the Corinthian church—they thought the gifts of the Spirit could be employed as a badge of spirituality. In my book, *Gifts of the Spirit for a New Generation* (Zadok Publishing, 2015), I suggest an altogether different purpose and operation of the gifts.

Losing Sight of the Main Thing

If we don't really believe we can get to the main thing, we will substitute it for secondary things. This is really the story of the entire Old Covenant. The children of Israel had turned away from God so many times (and then repented for a season), that they eventually replaced a relationship with the One True God with secondary things. They wanted a king like

If you make Scripture the highest form of worship, then you mistake tutors and educators for fathers. the other nations had instead of hearing God's voice. They settled for alliances with the other nations and inter-married with foreign wives rather than being a set apart people. Please don't misunderstand me; this was not uniquely Jewish, but the way of all humanity. But by the time Jesus arrived on the scene they didn't even recognize that Messiah had come. Jesus's own indictment against the religious leaders of Israel was that they searched the Scriptures but couldn't see the One the Scriptures promised. He said, "You search the Scriptures for in them you think you have eternal life, and these are they which testify of Me. But you are not willing to come to Me that you may have life" (John 5:39-40).

Sometimes the disappointments of life, things not turning out the way we thought they would, cause us to settle for secondary things. Sometimes we just can't believe that it could be that good. The leaders of Israel had tried to make several leaders into their Messiah—every hundred years or so a likely candidate would come along. After getting it wrong a few times, one tends to play it safe and opt for something controllable and predictable. This is not foreign to us, you know. We have our current end-times prophets who keep telling us the date Jesus is coming, that the world is coming to an end, until that date comes and goes and they have to re-calculate.

In Jesus's day, they had opted for studying the Scriptures as the highest form of worship. If you make Scripture the highest form of worship, then you mistake tutors and educators for fathers. So, Jesus attempts to recalibrate the religious understanding by saying, "Call no man 'father'" (Matt 23:9). Rather than a relationship with the God of Creation, they had decided to analyze what He had said long ago. The results—they kept adding new laws, more detailed, more meticulous, more refined codes. Then came commentary on the laws and codes, then commentary on the commentaries. No wonder Jesus's teaching sounded so fresh and authoritative (Matt. 7:29). He didn't quote what the rabbis said about what the rabbis before them had said. He actually told His hearers what His Father was saying!

The Corinthians Lose Sight of the Main Thing

Paul had a lot of encouraging things to say to the Corinthian believers. They were enriched in everything in all utterance (prophecy and revelation), and knowledge, and didn't lack in any of the gifts of the Spirit (1 Cor. 1:4-6). But clearly, the big issues he had to address was that the main things, fellowshipping and encouraging one another in the overflowing love of Christ, had been replaced with comparison, self-promotion, and divisiveness.

Notice Paul's charge to the Corinthians about how they interpreted leadership gifts contentiously:

> *Now, this I say, that every one of you says, I am of Paul;*
> *and I of Apollos; and I of Cephas; and I of Christ. …*
> *whether Paul, or Apollos, or Cephas, or the world, or life,*
> *or death, or things present, or things to come; **all are yours**;*
> *And you are Christ's, and Christ is God's.*
>
> 1 Corinthians 1:12; 3:22-23

Paul appeals to them on the basis of who they are and what they already have: "all things are yours"! But they don't see it. They are taking each other to court, thinking that spiritual gifts are a sign of spiritual maturity, and not even sharing their food with those in the church that don't have enough to eat. Some are wearing their wealth to church and settling into cliques, which creates divisions.

They certainly had not caught the revelation that they are sons/daughters of God and "all things are yours." They don't realize that all believers are essential members of the same body and no one can say to another member, "I don't need you." You see, the orphan spirit will take those things freely given by God and turn them into measurements to promote or assure self-esteem.

The orphan spirit will take those things freely given by God and turn them into measurements to promote or assure self-esteem.

You Might Still Think Like an Orphan If …

* If you feel like you don't quite fit in some circles (… you've lost sight that you are directly connected to the Head).

- If you feel like you will become important someday when you have achieved certain benchmarks (… you've probably lost sight that "all things are already yours" and you have nothing to prove because you are connected to the Head).

- If you feel better about yourself because you drive a Beamer rather than a VW (… you might have forgotten that we are all connected to the Head).

- If you would rather "go to court" and be proven right than do what it takes to be in right-relationship with your brother (… you might have lost sight that we are all connected directly to the Head).

- If you promote the adulation of one leader over another or celebrate leaders as superstars (… settling for less than God intended each believer to be—directly connected to the Head).

- If you need a position, title, or crowd to prove that you are important (… you might have lost sight that you are directly connected to the Head).

- If you feel more spiritual because you can prophesy, preach or sing (… you might have lost sight that all members are directly connected to the Head).

- If you receive a prophetic word and then spend a lot of energy trying to "make it happen" (… you might have lost sight that you are directly connected to the Head—what He has promised, He will perform).

Could it be that we just struggle to believe that it could be this good? Do we settle for less because it sounds too good to be true? Could this be why the Apostle John says, "Now are we the sons of God, though it does not yet appear what we shall be..." (1 John 3:2)? Is it that we haven't seen sonship in its full bloom yet and are afraid it's just preacher-talk? Is this why Jesus is praying so that His disciples hear when He says,:

Father, I am praying that you would help them to know that the same way You and I are One, they are one … as You Father are in Me, and I in You, that they also may be one in Us.
John 17:21, 23

Could it be that this Kingdom thing is not really about best practices, high performers, and the gifted and talented, as much as it is about a revelation of our sonship—living and thinking like sons because we are in the Son? Could it be that what we need is a "Fathering Spirit?"

Restoring the Fathering Spirit

The 17th chapter of the Gospel of John is really the Lord's prayer: that we would be one with one another by being one with Him. It sounds like strange, muted speech to us because we are focused on everything else. In Malachi 4, God promised to send the spirit of Elijah. The Spirit of Elijah represents a fathering spirit. Elijah was a spiritual father to Elisha and other prophets. The schools of the prophets were born out of that fathering spirit. Do you remember what Elisha cried out as he watched Elijah go up in the chariot of fire? "My father! My father!" (2 Kings 2:12).

It should be sobering and insightful to us that the last words of the Old Covenant are about a curse of fatherlessness and a promise to send a "fathering spirit." Malachi says on behalf of the Lord:

> *I'm going to send upon you a fathering spirit (the spirit of Elijah),*
> *and I'm going to turn the hearts of the fathers to the children, and the*
> *hearts of the children to the fathers, lest I smite the earth with a curse.*
> Malachi 4:5-6 (my paraphrase)

And we have seen how our earth is under a curse of fatherlessness. The word of the Lord wasn't heard again after Malachi for another 300 years—what we call the Intertestamental Period—until John the Baptist begins to declare the Word of the Lord:

> *He will come in the spirit and power of Elijah ... make way for the Lord.*
> Luke 1:17

What is "the spirit and power of Elijah?" It is a fathering spirit—in other words, the awakening of an army of the sons of God—not orphans, not religious zealots, not just students of the Scripture, not just people who go to church on weekends, but men and women who know they are sons of God, and the ramifications of that sonship. In fact, it seems this stirring of the fathering spirit impacts all of creation, for Paul says:

> *Even creation groans waiting for the manifestation of the sons*
> *of God... and we even groan in ourselves* [for it].
>
> Romans 8:22-23

Is this stirring something in your spirit as it is mine right now?

Spoiler Alert

Allow me to go ahead and connect the dots here. The Spirit of Elijah was a fathering spirit but manifested in signs, wonders, and miracles. How did Elijah do those miracles? The Holy Spirit would come upon him. What did Elijah's spiritual son, Elisha, do with the fathering he received? He did twice the miracles of his father, Elijah. Now to open the New Testament era, Jesus came up out of the River Jordan filled with the Holy Spirit without measure and began to do the same things Elijah had done, only more. And Luke writes in no uncertain terms that everything Jesus did, He did by the power of the Holy Spirit:

> *How Jesus was anointed with the Holy Spirit and with power,*
> *who went about doing good and healing all that were sick*
> *and oppressed of the devil, for God was with Him.*
>
> Acts 10:38

Isn't it interesting that at the same moment that Jesus is being filled with the Spirit the heavens open and He hears the Father's voice? Wait; let me say it again: at the same time Jesus is being filled with the Spirit the Father is speaking sonship saying:

> *This is my beloved son in whom I am well pleased!*
>
> Luke 3:22

Ah, there is a connection between Holy Spirit-fullness, the Father's voice, and sonship—this is the *Abba Cry.* (We explore the depths of this connection between Spirit-fullness, the Father's voice, and sonship in the sequel book *The Abba Formation.*)

Watch how the Old Testament closes, and the New Testament opens; it may just say something to us about what "the main thing" really is.

The Old Testament closes with Malachi saying "Fatherlessness (i.e., the orphan spirit) is the curse the earth is under, but I'm going to remove the curse by sending the fathering spirit." The New Testament opens (the effective launching of Jesus's ministry) with the Holy Spirit coming upon Jesus—Jesus hears an affirmation of His sonship—and is immediately rushed to the wilderness where every temptation He encounters is an attempt to create doubts about His sonship! *"If you be the Son of God*, command these stones be turned to bread. *If you be the son of God*, cast yourself off the Temple.

> **Jesus came to partner with the Holy Spirit to show us what happens when sons know who they are and simply live in the Father's love and presence.**

If you be the Son of God ...." Satan taunts. But there is a Spirit upon Jesus now— He has always been the Son of God, but now there is a Fathering Spirit upon a Man. Something has opened up now that changes everything!

By the way, every temptation you will ever face will be about the same thing—to steal the identity of your sonship—to separate you from the Father's love. Even at the end of Jesus's earthly ministry—He is hanging on the cross and people are walking by, wagging their heads and saying, "If you be the Son of God come down off that cross ..."(see Matt 27). Every temptation you will ever face, to the end of your life, will be about your identity as a son. You might as well get a revelation of this reality now.

This Is the Main Thing

Jesus has not just come to be a deliverer from Roman rule, or a Messianic hope for the people of Israel (though He certainly fulfilled that), or even to just take our sins away on a cross (though He certainly did that and we are forever grateful).[17] Jesus came to partner with the Holy Spirit to show us what happens when sons know who they are and simply live in the Father's love and presence. When the sons and daughters of God attend to everything the Father says, they are released to take their place in a partnership that will eventually see all the enemies of God under Jesus's feet and the kingdoms of this world delivered back to the Father.

This is why, after Jesus's resurrection, He says:

> *It is expedient for you that I go away ... so the Holy Spirit can come to you*
> *... and the same works that I have done, you will do*
> *and even greater works that these will you do.*
>
> John 14:12

When Jesus says this, He is connecting His ministry by the Holy Spirit to the fathering spirit of Elijah. He is saying, "The same way Elisha did twice the miracles Elijah did (the multiplication of fathering), you are going to do even greater works (in global and cultural impact) than Mine."

The *Abba Cry* is more than you and I getting a little stronger (though that is inevitable), more than getting free from some addictions (though that will be glorious), more than making you super-religious (we hope that never happens). The *Abba Cry* is about you being filled with a Fathering Spirit that drives out the orphan spirit and daily confirms in you, *"This is My beloved son/daughter, in whom I am well pleased."* This is about manifesting the works of God and destroying the works of the devil. This is about fulfilling our place as sons of God.

When you watch Jesus teach His disciples and do ministry with a Fathering Spirit for three and a half years, the things He says and does begin to take on a new shape. Let's fast-forward to the last hours He has with His disciples before His crucifixion and see this Fathering Spirit at work in what is commonly called "the Lord's Supper" or "the Last Discourse."

First, a quick overview of John 13-17 reveals that Jesus is focused on two things; going back to the Father, and introducing them to the Holy Spirit, who would come to them and carry on what Jesus has started. That's His focus—the Father and the Spirit.

Does it seem as startling to you as it does to me that Jesus refers to His Father fifty-eight times in this one evening with His disciples? Think about this. Jesus knows His hour has come—He is about to be betrayed, put through a mock trial, scourged, beaten beyond recognition, then hung on a cross. He has invested His whole ministry into these men, now only eleven. But He is not rehearsing the great crowds that attended His teaching, or the outstanding miracles, walking on water or Lazarus raised from the dead. All the things men would talk about if they were concerned about their legacy seem to be ignored. He is talking about His Father. He is talking about how everything the Father has belongs to Him, and that by this Holy Spirit, everything He receives from the Father will be available to His disciples (John 16:15).

This is the Fathering Spirit at work to transform orphans to sons and to release a movement of sonship upon the orphan planet. In fact, He speaks so much of the Father around the table that Philip seems exasperated and says:

"Lord, show us the Father, and it is sufficient for us."
John 14:8

This is the Fathering Spirit at work to transform orphans to sons and to release a movement of sonship upon the orphan planet.

I applaud Philip. At least Philip understood that Father was/is the issue. The main thing is not being right (keeping laws), but being rightly-related to the Father. Some haven't seen it yet.

Jesus said to him, "Have I been with you so long, and yet you have not known Me, Philip? He who has seen Me has seen the Father; or how can you say, 'Show us the Father'? Do you not believe that I am in the Father and the Father in Me? The words that I speak to you I do not speak on My own authority, but the Father who dwells in Me does the works. Believe Me that I am in the Father and the Father in Me, or else believe Me for the sake of the works themselves.
John 14:9-12

Jesus says, "My whole life is not about doing My thing or being somebody, but My life is about pleasing the Father."

And what is our life about? Is it about making a mark, leaving a legacy, being somebody, getting a name, being known as a great leader or a great businessman? Jesus says, "All of that is from an orphan spirit. What is important is that you know the Father and that you find out who you are as a son."

What's amazing to me as I pour through the words of this Last Supper, is that Jesus says over and over again, "I'm in My Father, and My Father is in me. We are one" (John 13:14). But then He begins to talk about a vine and includes you and me in this divine oneness (John 15), then He tells us how to join in the Triune conversation and mission of God by the Spirit (John 16), and then prays the main thing again:

"My prayer is that you would be in me and I in you, and we would be one in our Father."

In His great prayer both for those disciples and "for those who shall believe on Me," He asks the Father to give His disciples a revelation, not of unity, but identification and union.

59

"My prayer is that you would be in Me and I in you, and we would be one in our Father."

"That they might know that the same way I am in You (Father)*, and You are in Me, they will be in us."*

That's union. And this is the main thing. This is what Holy Spirit is doing in you and me right now. He is awakening us to the reality that old things have already passed away, and all things have become new. We are not just followers of Jesus, we are in Him, in union with Him, and He is in union with us. As a "follower of Jesus" we decide how close or how far behind we want to follow—but in *union*, there is no distance.

How can you and I be in union with Jesus, the Son of God, and not be on the Holy Spirit's radar? The Fathering Spirit, the Holy Spirit, is convincing us from the inside out that "now, we are the sons of God," and how sons think and live. This is the *Abba Cry*. In the next two chapters, we look more carefully at how we get drawn into the bondage of the orphan spirit, and the layers of orphan thinking that need to be removed from our consciousness.

What Have We Said?

We often miss the main thing that God has for us because we settle for secondary things; He sends His Son, but we settle for memorizing some Scriptures; we exchange the Person of Jesus for principles and precepts.

The orphan spirit will take those things freely given by God and turn them into measurements to self-promote or bolster self-esteem.

If we fail to realize we are one with the Head, who is Christ, we will settle for good performance, personal legacy, or best practices rather than a movement to recover the orphan planet.

The Old Testament ended with the curse of the orphan spirit upon the earth, but the New Testament era opens with the Fathering Spirit being released in the ministry of Jesus.

Jesus came as partner with the Holy Spirit to show us what happens when sons know who they are and how to live in the Father's love.

PRAYER

If the Lord is speaking to your heart would you open to His loving, gentle work and pray this with me?

Father, I see that there are two spirits warring for humanity. I see that though You led the people of Israel out of Egyptian slavery, it took longer to get the slave-mindset out of them. I understand believers can still have orphan thinking. Abba, would You show me where my thinking is more like the self-protecting orphan than like the free son? Would You show me if there are places where I think someone owes me something, or I am jealous because someone else has something I don't think I have. And, Lord, are there things that I have freely received from You that I have made the measure or symbol of my own success? Speak, and I will listen.

Thank You for sending the Fathering Spirit. Thank You for removing the curse of fatherlessness and its consequences of orphan thinking. Thank You for opening my eyes, and lovingly releasing the Abba Cry in my spirit that heals these deep wounds and begins to clear my thinking. Abba, I belong to You. I trust You. I love You. Amen.

Kerry Wood

GROUP DISCUSSION

1. What is the significance of the closing of the Old Testament and the opening of the New Testament with reference to "the spirit of Elijah?"

2. Which of the *"You might still think like an orphan if ..."* statements spoke to you the most?

3. Rabbinical teaching has asserted that "the highest form of worship is the study of Scripture." But why does the orphan mindset tend to replace the worship of the Person of Jesus with principles and precepts (see John 5:39-40)?

Five

The Progression to an Orphan Spirit

Lies are a little fortress; inside them you can feel safe and powerful.
Through your little fortress of lies you try to run your life
and manipulate others.

—Wm. Paul Young

Twelve-Step Progression

I am proud of you, dear reader, for continuing to behold His goodness. This is how lasting transformation happens. Let's keep going.

Terminology is important, and it is important to repeat at this point what I do and do not mean by an "orphan spirit." I am not using "spirit" in this context as a demonic spirit or the human spirit. I am using the term to refer to a prevailing attitude or mindset, much like Paul uses the term in Ephesians 4:23, "and be renewed in the spirit of your mind." Therefore, to have an orphan spirit does not necessarily mean a demon needs to be cast out, rather, the Holy Spirit needs to bring revelation into one's spirit that produces a freedom in one's believing and thinking. Likewise, a spirit of sonship is a revelation by the Holy Spirit in a believer's spirit that yields a new way of thinking and believing. More importantly, the Holy Spirit brings you to a new way to "be," more than just new ways to behave. The new way to be (from the inside out) inherently carries the new way to think and do.

You might be asking, "Why do I need to understand the progression of the orphan spirit? Why can't I just by-pass the details, get full of God, and let the Holy Spirit deal with the impacts of these stages? In short, it is because God has chosen union, to be united, one with us, and in that oneness, He sovereignly limits Himself to partnership with us. He chooses to work in partnership, working where we invite Him to work and as we are ready to receive what He wants to do. So, an awareness of the kinds of bondage and the entry points the enemy uses helps us to spot the

The Holy Spirit brings you to a new way to be, more than just new ways to behave.

residual effects and invite Holy Spirit to come at the point of our need. It also helps us to know how to guard against such enemy tactics in the future.

Understanding the progression of the orphan spirit can be a powerful tool for the Holy Spirit to begin to expose the enemy's lies that we have believed. This progression could be articulated in a variety of ways, but let's look at twelve possible factors.[18] As you read, ask the Lord to show you if any of these steps have found any root in your own life. In reality, we are all in the same boat and have to deal with most all of these at some time or another. These are the giants that are in your land. Let's take them down.

1. Failed Expectations: A focus on the faults of those who are in authority.

This usually begins at a very young age—often it is the simple mistakes of parenting that the enemy uses as *entry points* to sow lies into our thinking upon which strongholds will be built. Sometimes it is through traumatic experiences, accidents, pain, or molestation that Satan uses to imbed fear, resentment against others (especially those in authority), and rejection.

As we saw earlier, Lucifer's first words to Adam and Eve were said to get them to think the Father had made a mistake. He implied that Father hadn't given them everything—He had withheld some knowledge. "If you eat of this tree you shall not surely die … you will be like God." The fact was, they were already like God, made uniquely in His image.

Though you may have grown up with great parents, and in a godly home, every parent is a human being with faults. The Scriptures acknowledge the frailty of human parenting and the fact that, generally speaking, even the best of parents can only operate with what they received from their parents (Heb. 12:9). The father of orphans, Satan, wants you to focus on the fault, rather than the love of your parents, and begin to ask questions in your heart, "Why do I have to do it your way? Why can't I do what I want?" The orphan spirit wants you to focus on the failures, the frailties of those in authority over you. And if you don't learn to focus on the love rather than the fault of the parent, a root of bitterness and mistrust will spring up. Eventually, that mistrust of authority gets projected onto other authorities and it's not long before that person is jumping from one job to another, and one church to another.

Have you ever seen a person who keeps getting drawn to those jobs that have "sorry" bosses, and you wonder when they are ever going to get a job that has a good boss? In many cases, it is not the boss or the job, but something on the inside of the person that needs to be healed—a resentment or rebellion to authority, an inner vow or judgment that was rooted early in life. If you focus on the faults of those in authority, you'll never stay in one place very long. The Holy Spirit knows how to deal with that if you will ask Him. This is bigger than we think. We don't realize that Satan looks for ways to focus our attention on the pain, the disappointment, and reinterpret those wounds as personal rejection.

You might want to stop right now and ask, *"Holy Spirit, is there a root of bitterness or rejection in me due to unforgiveness toward authorities in my life? Are there unresolved issues, perhaps even subconscious ones, that You want to deal with in my life? I give You permission to bring anything to the surface that I need to renounce or of which to repent about authorities, in Jesus's name."*

2. **Personalized Rejection:** Receiving the faults of our leaders as either discouragement or rejection of self opens the door to a life of "wrong conclusions" about the evidence of our lives.

The sons and daughters that are brought up in a household of love may be disappointed or discouraged, but they still feel their parents' love and approval. What the enemy wants to do is to misinterpret a human mistake as a personal rejection. He will whisper in your ear, sow a suspicious thought about someone that you are supposed to trust.

Here's how this works: Your little boy comes running to you, and all he wants to do is jump in his father's arms, but he is totally unaware that you are holding a pair of scissors, or fingernail clippers. He jumps up and causes you to cut your finger, and just out of sheer reaction you move away from him instead of catching him in your arms. And your reaction, human frailty really, gets interpreted by that little boy as rejection.

When my first-born son was just a little guy, I came home exhausted from a long days' work, laid down on the living-room floor on my back, and within twenty seconds I was "out," taking a power nap. I didn't even think to take off my glasses. My little Robert discovered Daddy was home, and on the living room floor, which to his little mind meant that it was time to wrestle! I was sound asleep when he jumped right on my chest, smashing my glasses on my face (cutting the bridge of my nose), and I woke up with sharp pain running through my face and adrenaline shooting through my veins. I was in involuntary defense mode!

There was no intention in my heart to reject my son.

What do you do in defense mode? You throw off the aggressor! I woke up seeing my small son flying across the room! Fortunately, he landed on the couch; but unfortunately, I was the one who launched him!

At first, he thought I was playing with him (and he was ready to "do it again, Daddy"), then he realized I was hurt and had thrust him away from me. *There was no intention in my heart to reject my son,* but something that was completely innocent on my part could be interpreted by a son or a daughter as personal rejection. And the enemy wants to use that as an entry point for the seeds of an orphan spirit.

I wonder if anything happened in your childhood that was totally unintentional? Perhaps somebody did something, or said something out of human reaction, but it felt like rejection to you. The orphan spirit gains a place. We must remember that children are good observers, but not good interpreters. They see everything, but need help in properly interpreting what it means.

If you choose to focus on the love of a father or mother, even when that parent makes a mistake, you may feel disappointed, but that disappointment does not have to be an entry point for a lie or stronghold. If we choose to focus on their faults, their mistake will be received as a personal rejection. Why is this critical? Because the precious thing Satan is after is your sense of identity. If he can get you to believe you are rejected, he will try to interpret for you why you were rejected, ultimately to build a case against the Father's love.

Isn't it interesting that young ladies that don't receive a father's love become vulnerable (as we all do) for that love-need to be filled? We all need to feel loved, valuable, and special. What kind of a guy does a love-starved girl tend to attract? The kind that has learned to say, "I love you" and then abuse them. The same happens to guys, of course. Boys want their father's attention and approval. Dad is every boy's hero until he is rejected, berated, embarrassed, or worse yet, ignored. Dads that never received hugs don't just go to "hugs class" and learn how to hug. Something has to be healed inside. Hurt people hurt people. People that never hear, "I love you" as a child have a difficult time saying, "I love you" to their own children.

How many relationships are formed by an orphan attraction, with neither person knowing their true identity or the Father's voice? Without a felt awareness of the parents' love, the only option left our sons or daughters is to grasp for anything that will compensate for what they believe they lack. What I have sketched here is a generalization, of course, but repeated a million times over with slight variations. What happens when the girl (lacking a father's loving affection) keeps getting abusive guys (who readily offer that affection), and guys are told they can fill their emotional tank with sexual escapades to prove they are a man? Both become wounded and lose trust.

Is Holy Spirit saying anything to you, bringing any memories up that you want to offer to Him to heal, to forgive, to offer forgiveness?

3. Loss of Trust: We lose basic trust in others and begin to assume "everyone is the same."

Here's a simple example about a loss of basic trust. I get really excited when I'm speaking. If while teaching, I am walking back and forth, and accidentally step on someone's toe, that person probably wouldn't take it as rejection and lose trust in my character. They might think I am just clumsy. They might initially assume it was an accident. But what if, while this person's toe is still throbbing, I step close to his foot again? His immediate reaction is going to be to move that toe! If I continue to step close to his foot, totally unaware, he may develop doubts that I have his best interest in mind. This is about basic trust, and there's a difference between basic trust and deep trust. Basic trust lives where we know our best interests are important to others. But when one experiences the normal bumps and bruises of life, one learns to withdraw to protect. One becomes more and more hesitant to open up, to leave himself vulnerable, as before. We start living with our feet pulled back under the table.

Recognize that putting up emotional walls and keeping emotional distance is not something a young child knows to do. This is something we learn through the hard knocks of life. We get our toes stepped on a few times and we learn to self-protect. The good news is, the Holy Spirit is working to restore you to child-like trust.

Sigmund Freud has long been revered as the father of Psychology. But the emotional wounds from his father and the resulting resentment produced such lack of trust that it impacted the rest of his life (and undoubtedly colored his theories). His granddaughter, Sophie Freud, recounts that her grandfather, Sigmund, linked his fear of poverty to his father's lack of success. Sigmund's father was without work for most of the years of the boy's childhood. But Sigmund would recount one disturbing memory which revealed his tangled feelings and mistrust toward his father. When Freud was ten, his father, Jacob, had told him a story:

"When I was a young man, I went for a walk one Saturday... I was well dressed, and had a new fur cap on my head. A Christian came up to me and with a single blow knocked off my cap into the mud and shouted: 'Jew!'"

Young Freud interrupted, "And what did you do?"

Sigmund's father said, "I picked up my cap and walked away."

This was a major disappointment for young Freud. He was hoping his father would have done something dramatic and powerful, fought for himself, or defended his good name. Freud wanted a father who was strong, not someone who was submissive. Freud lost respect for his father, and shelved his Jewish faith.[19]

The enemy has been studying humanity for a few millennia; he knows how to reinterpret our story to us in such a way that we lose trust in those who love us.

4. Fear of Lack: Fear of failed provision, fear of not receiving comfort, love and affirmation.

If we begin to believe that people want to step on our toes, we respond by keeping a little distance. This is called fear: fear of hurt, fear of rejection. It might be more acute like Sigmund Freud, left with an abiding fear of scarcity due to his father's long-term unemployment. Where does this fear lead? Eventually we become fearful of receiving from others—even if what they are giving is love. When someone wants to give love, care, and compassion to us, we can no longer receive it. We reinterpret it through our mental/emotional script that tells us that people are not really looking out for us, and we reject it. Somebody says, "You did really well" or "You look really nice," and we respond in ways to minimize their words. "Oh, I bought this on sale ..."

Have you noticed that the people who are the most talented are often the most tempted to buy into the lie that they cannot do enough, or cannot be enough? Have you known someone who is artistic and incredibly talented? Have you noticed how the Van Goghs, Michael Jacksons, Robin Williams, Princes, and Whitney Houstons of the world struggle the most with self-doubt, insecurity, and identity? First, they feel "different" from everyone else, then celebrated, then suspicious because they can't know if their friends are real friends or just leaches, then they become deeply depressed.

Orphans lack an irreducible center— the core meaning of everything, and an identity rooted in something bigger than themselves.

Many will simultaneously feel entitled, then lost when the crowds fade, or they just feel used by the public for fascination and entertainment. Their life becomes a roller coaster of emotions, fears, loves and hates—they lack an irreducible center—the core meaning of everything, and an identity rooted in something bigger than themselves.

Every human being needs provision—but it's more than food and clothes. We all need meaning and purpose. We all need challenge and good relationships. We were created for unconditional love, and all the money in Hollywood, Silicon Valley, or Wall Street can't buy that! Our culture's most artistic souls discover this in a stark and glaring reality. What do the superstars and celebrities do to compensate for their lost intimacy? They build gates around their homes and hire bodyguards. They keep their distance—and in smaller, less noticeable ways, so do we.

Do you worry about a lack of provision? Have you experienced times where it didn't seem as if your parents, spouse, or even God was looking out for you? Do you have a nagging fear that someday you might run out? What do you think Holy Spirit would want you to know about the Father's unconditional love and endless provision? Fathers understand that they don't need to tell their children more than they can comprehend—but they do want their children to know they don't need to worry. A good father loves his children to relax in his provision. Is there anything you need to talk to your Heavenly Father about (right now) before reading further?

5. Self-protection: Our spirit closes to others and we build fences.

Are you asking the Lord to speak to you as you consider these orphan characteristics?

Have you ever seen a child storm out of the room and slam the door behind them? Or someone who turns their back on another person as if to say, "I'm going to pretend you're not here?" That is body language for a closed spirit. Have you ever been around someone whose spirit is closed? They may be present in body, but absent in every other way. Have you ever experienced "the silent treatment"? What about the person who will not venture beyond the news, sports, and weather conversationally? They believe themselves to be introverts, but really they're simply wounded and their spirit is closed.

He knows how to lovingly bring us from a mad cry, to a sad cry, to an *Abba Cry*. There is a cultural belief in North America (and the West in general) that says that all adolescents are likely to go through a period of rebellion (automatically closed spirits). It doesn't have to be that way. Repentance is how closed hearts are opened again. It is a parent's responsibility to keep pressing in, with loving discipline, to knock on the door of our child's heart, to teach children how to be reconciled—how to be restored in trusting, tender child-likeness again. Are there "six simple steps" of cause and effect that always work? Probably not. But don't buy into the lie that there is a season where your child's heart is going to be closed automatically.

Most parents of small children know the difference between a child's mad cry and a sad cry. When a little child must be disciplined, often he will respond first with a mad cry (mad that he cannot have his own way); but with proper sensitivity in discipline, there comes a brokenness in the child's spirit—the mad cry turns to a sad cry—sad that he has displeased the parent. In the same way, God is constantly at work to open our spirit to Him. He knows how to lovingly bring us from a mad cry, to a sad cry … to an *Abba Cry*.

This is why correction and reconciliation are so prominent in the Scriptures. A closed spirit must be re-opened before God can bring the needed transformation. Repentance and affirmation is how the closed spirit is opened again. One of the significant dynamics of the orphan agenda is a closed spirit. When we close our spirits to others we settle for surface relationships. We give up on intimacy and replace it with counterfeit affections. We may even maintain our routines of worship—sing the songs, raise our hands—but our spirit is actually closed to God.

Before you read further, why not ask the Lord about your own condition right now? Would He say your spirit is open or closed? Ask Him and then quietly listen. What is the Lord saying to you? Can you think of ways that you insulate yourself from others? Do you protect yourself from getting too close? This is one step in the orphan spirit—it is not how sons thrive.

The next progression in the descent into the orphan spirit is an independent "I'll-just-do-it-myself"-spirit.

6. An independent spirit: We develop a self-reliant attitude because trust doesn't seem to be an option.

If our spirit remains closed to those around us, we will believe the lie that no one else is looking out for our best interest. Sometimes it is sold as "conventional wisdom"—we must protect ourselves from clumsy people that step on our toes, so we decide to look out for ourselves. This independent, self-reliant attitude stems from the belief that we cannot trust others for help—and we have plenty of stories to validate our position. "Look out for number one." It sounds good, but it is devastating to a person's spiritual and emotional health—and draws us deeper into the orphan spirit.

We live in a broken world, raised by imperfect parents, with an enemy that roams about seeking to turn hurts into strongholds, to reinterpret life-events with his lie, to rob every person of their true identity in God. Add to the equation that "hurt people hurt people," and much of the devastation is almost automatic. We hear, "Daddy told me I was stupid and I would never be able to hold down a good job, so I'll just show him." Or, "Mamma said I was no good. I will just show her." Do you hear the independent, self-reliant attitude?

A Boy Named Lee

In 1939 a baby boy was born two months after his daddy died. He grew up without the voice of a father, placed in an orphanage during his early childhood before being reunited with his mother. He and his brothers constantly heard their now re-married mother say, "You are a burden. If it weren't for you, I could get somewhere. If I didn't have to lug you kids around and find food to feed you, I could do something."[20]

That little lad grew up with an orphan heart and a lie spoken into his identity that he was worthless. He chose early on that he would prove to his mother he was somebody special, and that he was not a burden. (Every child starts with innate dreams of being special; no one dreams of being average.) But he was raised in a culture and mentality that no one is special—and everyone around him seemingly reinforced the lie that he was no different. So he went into the marines and received training as a marksman. He bought into a lie that "If I am not special, then nobody else is either."

On a cool morning in November, 1963, he climbed the stairs of the Book Depository building in Dallas, Texas, and assassinated the President of the United States. Why? Because he wanted to be somebody. He wanted

Jesus doesn't come to condemn the self-reliant, but to speak to the wounds that the self-reliant are hiding. to prove to the world that he was special and his name would be remembered forever: Lee Harvey Oswald. This story is repeated over and over, only with different names and scenarios.

The orphan spirit wants to snuff out anything that looks like sonship—anyone that looks special. *The self-reliant attitude is really the counterfeit, the cover-up of a broken heart.* A self-made man is usually a good example of poor craftsmanship. Jesus doesn't come to condemn the self-reliant, but to speak to the wounds that the self-reliant are hiding. "A bruised reed he will not break" (Matt. 12:20). An independent spirit naturally fosters a bent toward control.

7. **Controlling Relationships:** We manipulate and manage our relationships for self-protection and/or personal advancement.

Self-reliance (usually a disguise for woundedness) requires careful management of relationships. We start holding one another at a distance, and choosing very carefully with whom we will associate. And the sub-conscious goal is to make sure we can control the relationship, even if the control is associating with someone who will mete out the abuse we believe we deserve. In other words, we don't let anybody in emotionally unless they come on our terms, even if our terms are broken and illogical.

Have you noticed that a culture of brokenness requires an acceptable language for calling the brokenness "normal"? We redefine our woundedness as "conventional wisdom" or common sense. An orphan's system of personal protection looks like wisdom to other orphans. *Self-protection is deemed as "best practices" in an orphan world.* We say, "Look out for number one" and "Be careful who you associate with." It's accepted as a truism. "If you want it done right, do it yourself." "It's lonely at the top (so get used to it)." But Jesus broke all those rules. He associated with people we are taught not to associate with, and was so whole in Himself, so secure in His identity, that others' brokenness didn't threaten Him. He had no fear that others' brokenness would get on Him or contaminate

Self-protection is deemed as "best practices" in an orphan world. Him; who He was and what He had was greater. And it drove religious folks nuts.

We only have to manage and manipulate relationships if we feel powerless in ourselves. But there is no "relax" button in the orphan spirit. If I am afraid that I cannot control others, or that I might be hurt again, what is the logical next step? We will take that up in the next chapter, but perhaps we need to ask Holy Spirit to talk to us about whether or not we only relate to people we can control or carry an independent spirit.

What Have We Said?

A person with an orphan spirit has no trust or faith to let others meet their needs. We can't put our lives in the hands of anybody else who would love us or care for us because we don't trust them. We feel like we have to achieve everything by ourselves.

The opposite work of the same spirit is to feel everyone owes me something. The orphan spirit seeks to control, manipulate and take from anyone who demonstrates sonship—that is, anyone who walks in a sense of ownership or authority becomes the target of the orphan spirit; the orphan spirit tries to get a hold of something that the son has.

The orphan spirit lives in anxiety, guilt and a sense of homelessness. A sense that one doesn't fit, that one doesn't have a place, or that everything must be earned, a position must be attained, in order to carve out one's own place.

Failed expectations begin at a very early age and can set us up for a sense of personal rejection. We lose trust in others, develop a fear of lack, then self-protect. The self-protection nurtures an independent spirit which teaches us to control our relationships. Does any of this sound familiar?

Prayer

Lord, what do You want to say to me about this? I'm listening. Amen.

GROUP DISCUSSION

1. If Satan's mode of operation is to re-interpret the events of your life into failed expectations, personal rejection, and loss of trust, what might that tell us about the Holy Spirit's role (See John 14:16-17)?

2. What does Sigmund Freud's story tell you about how misplaced expectations can open the door to strongholds?

3. What does Lee Harvey Oswald's story tell you about Satan's strategy to isolate us from others with an independent, self-reliant spirit?

Six

The Progression to an Orphan Spirit Continued

The cruelest lies are often told in silence.
—Robert Louis Stevenson

I realize this may feel very heavy but it is important to draw a clear contrast between these two mindsets—these two spirits (mindsets) that are warring against one another for the soul of humanity. If you can see clearly the ugly effects of the orphan heart, you will welcome the work of the Spirit to begin to shape something new in you that displaces the bondage of fear.

Perhaps it would be helpful to remind you here of why these issues and ever-increasing stages of brokenness and isolation are so anti-Christ and anti-Kingdom and not just personal preference.

To a Relational 3 and 1 God, Sin is a Break in Relations

God is by nature a Three-and-One God; three Persons of one essence. The Trinity defines not only the most fundamental nature of God, but how the rest of the universe is wired for relational wholeness. This means that you and I, created in God's image, are also three-and-one beings (spirit, soul and body—1 Thess. 5:23), and are most whole when we are wholly relational. So sin is best defined, not as bad behaviors, but as relational brokenness. The Ten Commandments themselves speak of wholeness in relationship—the first four commandments express relationship with God and the last six speak of right relationships with one another. If our relationships are whole, we won't be acting in ways that wound and isolate. (To get the more exhaustive explanation of relational wholeness as salvation see *The Abba Foundation* by Dr. Chiqui Wood, Burkhart Books, 2018.)

With God's nature of relational wholeness in view, let's look at the last five steps in the progression of the orphan spirit, with the understanding that Satan's real end-game is to "separate us from the Father's love" (Rom. 8:38-39).

Twelve-Step Progression Continued

8. Conditional and Superficial as Real: We settle for superficial relationships.

We are willing to settle for superficial relationships because we are afraid to open ourselves up to know or be known. One of the lies orphans believe (though subconsciously) is that they are excluded from the father's house because of something they did wrong. There must be something wrong with them, they deduce, and if anybody ever really knew them, they wouldn't accept them. The self-protective answer is to refuse to allow others in; so it's news, sports, weather, casual sex, a promiscuous lifestyle to attract attention on your own terms. It is the façade of personal power.

But in Father's house you can be a child again. You can play, and you can dance. In Father's house, even if you don't know how to dance, you can act like you can dance. You can make up your own dance. In Father's house you can dance in your pajamas. In Father's house you can lie around and eat ice cream and not have to perform to be accepted. In Father's house we know that our Heavenly Father knows us through and through and He still loves us. Bill Gaither said it like this, "The One who knows me best loves me the most."[21] In Father's house, sons and daughters can accept one another because they're all in on equal terms. There are no orphans, no nephews, no cousins or grandchildren. All are all brothers and sisters; sons and daughters.

If it sounds like I am advocating an undisciplined lifestyle, let me assure you that I am not. There is high productivity as partners in the Father's business, but it is not a productivity created by the necessity to prove something, but from an overflow of being somebody.

God has made us, who were former nobodies, in to His somebodies.
Romans 9:25 (The Message)

It is not a productivity created by the necessity to prove something, but from an overflow of being somebody.

The Church at some point in time must have had a deep revelation of what it means to be sons and daughters in Father's house. Historically, believers would call one another "brother" and "sister" (e.g. Acts 28:15; Rom. 1:13; 7:1, and dozens of references throughout the New Testament). We don't do that as much anymore; it sounds religious to us now, but the Church needs a breakthrough in a revelation of sonship again so that we know one another as sons and daughters whether we use the term or not. It means that we can be ourselves. It means that we can be open, and that we can dare trust one another. It means that we understand that God has put us in one another's lives because we need each other, and there's something we can share.

Superficial relationships are the antithesis of who God is as a Triune relational being of love. Superficial relationships are the opposite of what God desires for His children. But it is the way of the orphan spirit. And it becomes ingrained as normal.

Do you have trouble letting others in? Have you labelled yourself an "introvert" or a "loner", to give yourself a pass on relationships? Is there something the Holy Spirit wants to talk to you about right here? *Holy Spirit, is there something You want to heal in me so that I actually enjoy being with people and people enjoy being with me?* Stop and listen.

9. **The Thought Becomes a Stronghold:** Lies, once believed, move from thoughts to strongholds (James 1:14-15).

A stronghold thought convinces us that we are on our own. A stronghold thought that says "You are on your own" will drive you one of two directions: either to muscle-up to make a name for yourself (the victor), or to become co-dependent under the guise of entitlement (the victim).

The orphan spirit has produced countless billionaires and millionaires who are out to prove that the absent dad, the harassing teacher, or bullying brother of their childhood were wrong. The orphan spirit has also produced more homeless people, drop-outs and government dependents. No insensitivity is intentioned, my dear friend, but the reality is that the orphan spirit drives people because they don't know who they really are. Without a revelation of sonship via the Father's voice, we are all herded like cattle in a wasteland without water, seeking desperately to find a sense of significance but distracted by every hunger pain of the body and soul.

Once that stronghold thought, "I'm on my own," settles in and we begin to live life like a spiritual orphan, there may be help all around, but we don't see it. Our own lens blind us from the grace that is available. There may be somebody reaching out to provide for us, but we don't trust them, because orphans have to grasp, claw, and scrape for a sense of inheritance.

My prayer is that one day the Church will tire of ministry without relationship. Sometimes that grasping looks very noble: a great college education, prestigious titles, notoriety and lots of money.

Sons live a life of ease, as far as orphans are concerned, because they can just "be," and sooner or later they are going to get their inheritance. But orphans have no inheritance because they have no father, so they strive, self-promote and manipulate. Have you noticed that there is a lot of striving, manipulation and self-promotion, even in the Church? Have you noticed the social media posts describing how busy we are in the work of God? Do you see leaders "tweeting" how many frequent flier miles they've "earned" to go tell the Good News?

My prayer is that one day the Church will tire of ministry without relationship. I pray the day will come when ministers can't get away with travelling from place to place, operating in their gifts but without relationships; that we take to heart Paul's admonition to "know those who labor among you"(1 Thess. 5:12).

The orphan lie that one is "on his own" doesn't necessarily mean that a person has no relationships. He may have many relationships. The difference is that those relationships tend to be utilitarian—to fill a need, to accomplish a task, to reach a goal, even if the goal is to be well-connected. Those relationships tend to be valuable until the need is met or the goal is reached. Intimacy, genuine vulnerability to know and be known, is a foreign language to spiritual orphans. Once a person is ensnared in the stronghold, it only seems normal to fill the voids with something that feels good, looks good, or at least masks the pain.

10. Accepting the Counterfeit: We chase counterfeit affections.

The reality is, Satan has usurped temporary authority from Adam, and is called the god of this world (2 Cor. 4:4 KJV), and the prince of the power of the air (Eph. 2:2). He possesses limited power and authority. Since he is not God he cannot create, he is not omniscient (all-knowing), omnipresent (all-present), or omnipotent (all powerful), so his only real tool is deception. If he can get us to believe the lie that he has power, it is as though he does. And because he has some limited ability to manipulate the earth's atmosphere, he can play on people's five senses to try to validate his lies.

The next chapter, entitled "Fake Fullness," will address in more detail how Satan plays on man's five senses to "run a counterfeit scheme" that is very impressive. After all, he has had a few thousand years of watching and learning how humans give away their secrets, weaknesses, and fears. He is a roaring lion (using intimidation) to snare human souls through passions, possessions, position and power—whom we are commanded and empowered to resist steadfastly (1 Peter 5:8-9). These counterfeits are only alluring if we lack a revelation of our full inheritance and position as sons and daughters of God.

We can wake up as sons, empowered by the Spirit, appreciating a new day to climb into Father's lap and feel His heart, to find what His mission is, do whatever He tells us to do, and feel the joy of hearing His voice.

11. **Redefining the Terms:** False definitions are Satan's way of making right seem wrong and wrong seem right.

By this time in the progression toward an orphan spirit, a person has accepted false definitions about almost everything that is significant in their lives; false definitions of God, of themselves, of love, of what a meaningful life is meant to be. Here are some false definitions that the marketing industry perpetuates—mostly rooted in the lure of passions, position, possessions or power—to sell products. See if you recognize any of them:

"You only go around once, so go for the gusto."

Life is redefined by how much fun one has on the weekends.

"You deserve a break today, so get up and get away."

Every orphan is convinced that he/she is not getting what he "deserves" and that others are living a life they don't deserve. This is the prodigal son—taking his inheritance early. This is the rue of socialism and communism—that no one deserves more than another based on faithfulness, diligence, or initiative, so everyone deserves the same. These are the dreams of which credit cards are made. Speaking of credit cards …"Some things in life are priceless. For everything else there is Mastercard." There is nothing subtle about the idea of buy now, pay later for an orphan world.

The primary idea of marketing is to convince a person they need something they don't really need, and that possessing that thing will enhance or determine their identity. When absolute truth is exchanged for "perception as reality" it is relatively easy to redefine the worldview of the populace.

It is a known tactic in the revolutionary's handbook—to conquer any people one must either overpower them with sheer force of violence or win them over slowly by redefining their terms. Just in my lifetime, the terms have slowly been redefined. An unborn baby is now an "embryo" or "fetus." Addictions are now a "disease." Homosexuality, has morphed from a sin-stronghold to a birth abnormality, to lifestyle choice, to how one chooses to self-identify at the moment. Pornographic images are now called "explicit" or "adult content." Words that used to be vile and vulgar are now just "language." Adultery is casual or consensual sex. Theft and fraud are "working the system."

We can de-humanize our enemies, legitimize our vices, and sterilize our conscience by redefining the terms. This is how we "exchange the truth of God for a lie" (Rom 1:25). This is how we slowly progress into the orphan spirit and call it "going for the gusto." By putting a virtuous name on our sin, we strengthen the stronghold.[22]

12. A Life of Oppression: The high cost of low living which we come to call "life."

A life of oppression says, "I don't have what it takes. Everybody else gets blessed but me." The narcissistic world we live in boldly declares that a man can self-identify as a twelve-year old girl, or a giant lizard, or a moonbeam. And though most don't go to such extremes, humans go to great lengths to be the captain of their own ship.

This final step into the orphan spirit needs the least explanation; it is sadly prevalent throughout modern culture. The orphan life is re-defined as normal—it's the oxygen our world breaths and goes largely undetected. We have exchanged the truth of God for a lie. The orphan heart says "I'm on my own. I'll make it up as I go. I don't have a father, I don't have a home. We'll redefine the terms and call it "really living." For most, it's not so bizarre—it's just a life of mediocrity and

> **To conquer any people one must either overpower them with sheer force of violence or win them over slowly by redefining their terms.**

living far beneath what your Heavenly Father had planned for you. This is a life of oppression—the orphan life.

Do you remember the family in the red convertible Mustang? The family is driving through the most scenic wonderland of mountains, green pasturelands, beside a clear-water river. But only one member of the family is enjoying the view. The father dearly loves every member of the family. But one child is putting a smile on the father's face.

The Holy Spirit is tuning your ear to hear the Father saying:

> *"This gift, this promise is for you and your children, and all who are afar off—even as many as the Lord, our God shall call."*
>
> Acts 2:39

"Whoever shall call on the name of the Lord will be saved (Acts 2:21; Rom. 10:13)—saved from the lie, saved from death, saved from themselves. Draw near to Me and I will draw near to you."

I believe, in the depths of my being, that the Lord wants every son and daughter to thrive under His smile that says, "I've gifted you; I'm providing for you; I've called you, you belong to Me. You belong in My house. You will have what you need to have, when you need to have it. You will know what you need to know, when you need to know it. I am a Good Father, and I've made sure of that."

A Vision for His Church

I saw a church once where the pastor was smiling (that's not unusual because public people learn to smile). But this pastor was overflowing as he was talking about the different people in his church, and what God had done in their lives.

As he began to introduce me to one, and then to another and then another, I noticed something very unusual. The pastor was introducing his congregation to me one by one, telling me how wonderfully they fit in their place and excelled in their gifts, and they just beamed as he spoke about them. And then they'd reach over and kiss the pastor on the cheek. I thought, "That's different!" These were men kissing men on the cheek. The pastor would tell them how wonderful they were, and then they'd put their arms around each other and kiss each other on the cheek. I'd never seen this before.

Then he took me to the lobby and introduced me to several people lined up: custodians and janitors with their name on their work shirt. They all stood there and beamed as if I was some general walking by to bestow a national honor on the troops. And they beamed as the pastor introduced me to each of them by name. As they came toward me I would reach out my hand for a handshake, but they would walk past my hand, open their arms and embrace me. The janitors were hugging me and kissing me on the cheek. It was awesome and strange at the same time. Everywhere we went around that property, every person that we encountered would walk up to the pastor and give him a hug. The men would kiss him on the cheek. They were hugging me, and some of them kissing me on the cheek, and I would return that kiss.[23]

That church is my church. That is the church I see in my spirit. I see a church that is bathed in the Father's voice, where sons and daughters flourish under that Voice. They are not striving for position or name or accolade, but finding their place and their love in being with brothers and sisters. And every time they get together they are having an unforced party, like Italians looking for something to cook. They are looking for an excuse to get together, and when they do, they express their affection freely and properly, with no self-consciousness. And when these people come together in child-like innocence, it's a wonderfully contagious atmosphere.

My prayer is that God's mission and vision for our city—your city—would be fulfilled, and that He would use you in your part to fulfill His mission of bringing many sons to glory. How many would be captivated by the love they see among us!

I pray that if you see yourself somewhere in this progression of the orphan spirit, that even as you read this, the orphan spirit is being displaced by a Spirit of Adoption that cries out, *"Abba, Father!* I am a son! I don't have to prove anything to anyone! I don't have to have possessions, position, or power to be somebody. I am in Jesus, the Beloved."

What Have We Said?

We are willing to settle for superficial relationships because we've believed a lie that no one would love us if they really knew us.

That lie gets reinforced by self-fulfilling rejection of others which produces a stronghold that says, "I'm on my own"—self-reliance (or the other extreme is victimization).

We sooth the pain of our loneliness with counterfeit affections.

Those lies come with re-defined terms so that right seems wrong and wrong seems right.

PRAYER

Can I pray this for you?

Father, we love You. Jesus, You have made a way for us to come boldly. Holy Spirit, You want to vibrate through our inner being right now. Shape the "Abba, Father!" within this reader's heart right now, not just the words but the reality. Wash their mind, their mistraining, dispel lies that my friend has believed. Nothing washes our mind and frees our weary soul like Your voice, Abba, coming up from our spirit by the indwelling Holy Spirit. Daddy, my Father, let them hear Your response right now, "You are My beloved son. In you I am well pleased." Lord Jesus, thank You for opening the way by giving Yourself, that we can come before the Father. Thank You for opening the invitation to us all to cry "Abba, Father." As we continue on this journey, uproot every lie we have believed; deeply implant the truth, by the Holy Spirit. Make us free to stand up in the back seat, arms open wide, able to freely enjoy all You have prepared for us. Amen.

GROUP DISCUSSION

1. What does James 1:14-15 tell us about how strongholds get established in our lives?

2. What are some of the reasons we are willing to settle for superficial relationships when we are made for real intimacy?

3. How have you seen the stronghold thought that says, "I'm on my own," play out in different situations?

4. Name some ways we see the terms being redefined in our culture to make the strongholds of either self-reliance or victimization acceptable.

Seven

Fake Fullness:
Accepting Counterfeits as Real

For in Christ all the fullness of the Deity lives in bodily form, and in Christ you have been brought to fullness.
—Colossians 2:9-10 (NIV)

In the previous chapter, one of the steps of the orphan progression was "Accepting the Counterfeit"—chasing for counterfeit affections. Because it is such a common ploy of the enemy, and so much so that many consider it normal, it needs special attention. By now you see the clear contrast between the orphan spirit and sonship. It is in the light of Truth that the counterfeits become so apparent. When we don't know who we are, that we have all things at our disposal as sons of God, we try to fill the voids in numerous ways. Before we consider our tendencies to pretend sonship, let's rehearse the characteristics again using slightly different language.

The **Spirit of Sonship** (atmosphere of love) says:

- I have a Father who loves me.
- I belong.
- I don't have to perform to be loved.
- I'm a son/daughter.
- I have a home.
- I can be myself.
- Father knows me better than I know myself—and He loves me.
- Because I'm a son, I have an inheritance.

The **Orphan Spirit** (atmosphere of fear and bondage) says:

- I don't know who my father is.
- I must achieve, perform, and prove myself.
- I must earn my way into the family.
- I don't belong here, so I must be someone I am not.

- I don't know who my father is, and therefore, I don't know if I have an inheritance.
- Since I don't have an inheritance, I must claw and grab for everything I can get.
- I particularly aim at taking what belongs to sons, since they didn't do anything to deserve what they have.

God's Desire is Genuine Fullness

In order for us to recognize fake fullness, we need to establish what genuine fullness looks like. To do this, we go back to God's own way of being. God has never had a lonely day. Before He created anything, He enjoyed complete, satisfying, overflowing fullness within the fellowship of Himself—Father, Son and Holy Spirit. In fact, the first three verses of Scripture reveal the Triune God creating out of the abundance of this overflowing fellowship, not because They needed anything. "In the beginning *God* created … the *Spirit* hovered over the void … and the *Word* was spoken …." (Gen. 1:1-3).

A Trinitarian World

The Relational Nature of God is seen in everything He has made—the three-and-one nature of matter (solids, liquids, and gases), of the molecule (protons, electrons, neutrons), of color (variations of blue, yellow and red), of music and sound (three notes making the fundamental element of a chord, three chords as foundation for every song), geometrically the world is built on the three dimensions of the line, the square and the cube (length, height, and width). Physicists tell us now that the power of molecular structure is not so much about the three components of the atom, but the space between those components, that is, the relationship they share—and the dynamic gravitational pull.

Before He created anything, He enjoyed complete, satisfying, overflowing fullness within the fellowship of Himself.

But the crown jewel of creation is humanity—"Let us make man in our image …" (Gen 1:26). God made man as a triune being: spirit, soul, and body (1 Thess. 5:23). One of the many unavoidable certainties of being made in the divine image is that humans are wired to be in relationship. (To study deeper in this area, see *The Abba Foundation*.)

Humanity is becoming a genius at counterfeit connections and counterfeit affections.

Man Is Designed to Connect Through Worship

Every human being is designed to be connected. "It's not good for man to be alone" God said. Man was made in the image of the Three-and-One relational God, and hardwired for relationship. But humanity's fallenness has short-circuited the wiring of God's original design. So man insulates himself in mistrust, not deeply connected with another person. What is the consequence?

The very real consequence of our three-in-one nature is that humanity will connect with something through worship. Even if mankind refuses to worship and connect to God, he will find something, even if it's not the right thing, to worship in connectedness. This is not just a human option of many options; man, when in a healthy state, will connect with something or someone, even if it is a counterfeit connection. In fact, what we are observing in the current explosion of social media is that humanity is becoming a genius at counterfeit connections and counterfeit affections.

Another way to express this idea of being properly connected is *fullness* versus *emptiness*. Think about the gas gauge on the dashboard of your car. *Full* is good, *Empty* is bad. God has designed us to be full in emotional well-being, spiritual vitality, physical health, relational wholeness. His overflowing, other-centered nature created us to be filled with God Himself, so that we would know and experience life as God has it. Thus, one of the consistent themes running through the New Testament is fullness.

- Jesus was *filled* with the Spirit without measure (John 3:33-35)
- When Jesus multiplied loaves and fish He did so in a way that demonstrated the Father's desire to provide an abundance, "They ate and were all full, and had twelve baskets left over." (Mark 6:43)
- Jesus's first miracle wasn't about a life or death necessity, but gracious *abundance*, turning water into wine (John 2:1-11).
- Jesus granted a supernatural catch of fish for weary fishermen that demonstrated gracious *fullness*—until the boats nearly sank with abundance (John 21:11).

- After His resurrection Jesus ascended to the Father's Right Hand and poured out the Holy Spirit in *fullness* upon 120 disciples, then 3,000 and beyond (Acts 2:2-4).
- Paul prayed that all believers would be *filled* with all the fullness of God (Eph. 3:19), and
- Commands the believers to "be *filled* with the Spirit" (Eph. 5:18).

God created humanity to be relationally connected, and to enjoy a fullness of life through relationships. But He wants to be the source of our fullness. It brings Him joy to fill His children with all that we would need. It is the nature of every good father to want to be the source for his family. Jesus said:

> *Your heavenly Father knows what you need even before you ask Him ... seek Him as your source and all these things will be added to you.*
> Matthew 6:32-33, paraphrased

The Father wants you filled with what is real life and life-giving, as Jesus said:

> *I have come that you might have life, and have **it** to the **full**.*
> John 10:10, NIV

Satan's Strategy is Fake Fullness

Satan wants to lure us away from God as Source, so that we will opt for counterfeits. His real goal is to separate you from the love of God, so he offers counterfeit affections. In the food and nutrition world they refer to "empty calories." That cake or pie tastes, "oh, so good;" but there is no nutritional value to feed your body. It is fake food, fake fullness, or as Solomon called it, "deceptive foods" (Prov. 23:3, NASB). It's called deceptive because the negative results don't show up immediately; but if I keep going back to the fake food for fake-fullness, the results become evident in bulges and sags, tight clothes, and pounds of fat that are much more difficult to lose than to find.

This is how Satan works. He has studied humanity for a few thousand years now. He knows about the God-given desires that are built into man.

Achievement and productivity are God-given desires. Eating is God-given and an essential drive. Sexual desire is a God-given drive—and so is acceptance, power, the relationality of knowing and being known. But the enemy's scheme is to convince you

Every temptation you will ever face is aimed at your identity—to get you to doubt your sonship.

that God is not interested in one or two of those areas being "full" for you. Others have fullness in that area, but not you. "Why not?" Satan will whisper, "You deserve fullness in that area, too." And he lures us to believe that we will have to fill that part of our "needs tank" in our own way and by our own initiative.

Here are Two Realities of Our Spiritual Warfare:

1. Every temptation you will ever face will play on a God-given drive, thus easily rationalized.

Why did Abraham finally have a child by his concubine Hagar instead of waiting, when God had already said that the child would come through Sarah? Because the promise of a son was God-given. It is easy to rationalize that "God said it would happen, but it is not happening the way He said, so it must be OK to try another route." Every temptation you will ever face will play on a God-given drive—only with the slight twist—that God is not filling some appropriate need for you—"You're on your own" Satan whispers; and so we convince ourselves that we are helping God out and produce an Ishmael.

2. Every temptation you will ever face is aimed at your identity—to get you to doubt your sonship.

Do you remember Jesus's temptations in the wilderness? These temptations were real—but not really about physical hunger or Jesus's ability to perform miracles. They were about Jesus going somewhere besides the Father for His provision—or we could say, "counterfeit worship."

Every temptation you will ever face is not just about getting you to sin, but to doubt your sonship: that you have a Father who loves and cares for you perfectly, and knows what you need and when you need it. Satan is not just trying to "steal, kill and destroy" (John 10:10). Yes that is his mode of operation, but his real goal is to separate you from the Father's love—to get your worship.

Satan's two chief tactics are to isolate, then distort. If he can isolate you from the truth (he does this by breaking down relationships with angst, resentment, and unforgiveness), then he will misinterpret (distort) the events of your life so you will "look out for number one." Satan likes to isolate us (through broken or infected relationships) to get us alone with our thoughts, because that is where he can whisper lies to us about our identity. If we buy into the distortion, we will accept counterfeit affections to fill the longing for deep, intimate, God-created connection.

Counterfeit Affections

Counterfeit affections come in four different categories: passions, possessions, position, and power. Allow these to serve as gauges that reveal sonship or an orphan spirit. Ask the Holy Spirit to show you where these could be playing a role in your life. When He shines a light on something, don't get condemned about it, just turn it into a conversation with God—ask Him what to do about it—He will talk to you:

A) Passions of the Flesh

The first counterfeit affection plays on our natural God-given physical needs. Our five natural senses, connected to our neurological (nervous) system, constantly send messages to our brain that trigger chemical reactions—releases of "feel good" chemicals of endorphins, enkephalins and adrenalines. We don't realize that when certain persons smile at us, it sends a message to our brain that releases a tiny chemical reaction that either feels good or bad. Scientific studies are now showing that we get small drips of "feel good juice" when we see that someone "likes" our Facebook post. (Could this be why people sitting together at the coffee shop are not talking to one another, but checking their phones for social media updates? They aren't getting their buzz from their in-person friends, so they are looking for the caffeine of a "like.") These dopamine releases are very addictive. It's how habits are formed.

Do you know why sex is such a powerful attraction? Because God designed our bodies to release a huge rush of endorphins as a result of sexual intercourse so that we would be forever bonded emotionally and neurologically to our spouse. This is why He commanded us to only have intercourse within the bounds of marriage.

> *The man will leave his father and mother, and the two shall become one flesh.*
> Genesis 2:24

Every human being was created for fullness. Every person was created to be connected spirit to Spirit—as son to Father—and to never lack anything we would ever need.

He designed spouses to bond physically, emotionally, psychological, and spiritually. He also knew that extramarital or recreational intercourse would release chemical and emotional bonding to a person with which we were not spiritually "one." What a trap! The results could be massive confusion in the emotional and psychological integration of a person. Pornography is particularly debilitating—its lure is an at-will chemical rush without the work of relational engagement and self-giving that is required in loving human connection. The disconnect that happens to our real relationships are lethal. We are deriving our "feel good" from taking rather than giving. Think about how this has conditioned an orphan world. God's commandments are never about restriction to our fulfillment, but to keep us from "fake-fullness" that eventually destroys us.

Created for Fullness

Every human being was created for fullness. Every person was created to be connected spirit to Spirit—as son to Father—and to never lack anything we would ever need. Every one of us was created for a comfort zone called "the Father's house." Every one of us was created to be wedded to something, and if we don't feel connected to something or someone, we will opt in to anything that makes us feel valuable and visible.

If husbands (or wives) are getting more "likes" at the office than they are at home, guess where they will want to spend most of their time? They become neurologically and chemically conditioned. Fathers, if your sons and daughters don't feel your heart and your unconditional love, it won't be long until they run for superficial, counterfeit affections to fill that void, because they are wired internally to be emotionally connected somewhere.

This is also why fashion and self-image are such powerful drivers. If I am in shape, handsome, and receiving "likes" (compliments and attention) from people who see me, I am receiving regular drips of chemical rush to my neurological system which make me feel good. Image, especially in our "selfie" world, has become a chemical addiction that is as prevalent in the Church as well as outside it. (Please read *The Abba Formation*, Burkhart Books, 2018 to see how experiencing the transformational work of the Holy Spirit in our lives can re-wire these addictions.)

B) Possessions

God is not against possessions. He is the original Owner and possesses it all. He is also the winner of all competitions of generosity, so He is not a Scrooge or a Grinch. He wants His children to have all they need and more—not just so they have no worries, but so they know who their Father is. But He doesn't want those possessions displacing their love for the Father. He knows how easily we can shift our attention from the Source to the resource. This is why He warns the people of Israel about the dangers of the blessings that He is sending their way:

> *For the Lord your God is bringing you into a good land, a land of*
> *brooks of water, of fountains and springs, that flow out of valleys*
> *and hills; a land of wheat and barley, of vines and fig trees*
> *and pomegranates, a land of olive oil and honey; a land in which you*
> *will eat bread without scarcity, in which you will lack nothing;*
> *a land whose stones are iron and out of whose hills you can dig*
> *copper. When you have eaten and are full, then you shall bless*
> *the Lord your God for the good land which He has given you.*
> *Beware that you do not forget the Lord your God by not keeping*
> *His commandments, His judgments, and His statutes which I*
> *command you today, lest—when you have eaten and are full,*
> *and have built beautiful houses and dwell in them; and when your*
> *herds and your flocks multiply, and your silver and your gold are*
> *multiplied, and all that you have is multiplied; when your heart is*
> *lifted up, and you forget the Lord your God who brought you out of*
> *the land of Egypt.*
> Deuteronomy 8:7-14

God is not against fullness; He is the creator and provider of it. Every good and perfect gift comes from Him (James 1:17). But He warns us that there are counterfeit affections. Jesus clearly revealed, "He (the Father) knows what you need even before you ask" (Matt. 6:32-33). Unfortunately, if we don't know our Father, we will seek possessions as substitute for relationship with Abba. Jesus said that our love of the Father could not be in competition for a love of wealth or the symbols of it (Luke 16:13).

One of the diabolical temptations of the enemy is to get us to anesthetize the pain of our identity crisis with *"stuff."*

One of the diabolical temptations of the enemy is to get us to anesthetize the pain of our identity crisis with *"stuff."* We have learned to substitute a connection with people by connection with things. This is called idolatry. The symbols of success play on the identities of church-goers and non-church folks alike.

A man cursed me one day for touching his Ferrari (OK, I shouldn't have touched it, but it was at an auto show!). Do you think that symbol of success might have been tied to his sense of identity and self-esteem? Do you know anyone who has gone into debt, put themselves under the daily pressures of paying exorbitant monthly interest payments, so they could feel better about themselves by wearing, driving, or living in something that looked like success? We insulate ourselves with stuff and think that we're important, because we have everything a son has. But it's only surface level. We are addicted to the "chemical drips" of the approval of others.

True worship will satisfy us in the deepest ways, without the exorbitant taxes, interest payments, or hang-overs. When we get full in spirit, we discover the greatest freedom is having nothing to prove. Paul had discovered the freedom that comes in sonship. He says:

I know how to be abased, and I know how to abound. Everywhere and in all things I have learned both to be full and to be hungry, both to abound and to suffer need.

Philippians 4:12

One translation says, "I have learned to be independent of my circumstances." Jesus demonstrated that He could live like a servant, not even having a place to lay His head, because He knew who He was in His Father's love (John

When we get full in spirit, we discover the greatest freedom is having nothing to prove.

13:3-5). This is a practical difference between the spirit of sonship and the orphan spirit. It includes being able to feel just as good about oneself driving an older economy car with high mileage, as driving a new luxury car.

How Does Luxury Make You Feel?

During my first pastorate we had two cars, a 1968 Ford Fairlane and a newer (but not brand new) Chrysler Cordoba. Then someone gave us a relatively new baby-blue Cadillac Seville, with white leather Landau top and white leather seats. It was beautiful and all luxury. Of course, one of the church members quickly told me the devil gave it to me. But actually, God used it not only to bless my family, but to teach me something about myself.

I realized one day that I sat up straighter and felt more confident driving the Cadillac, and when I would drive the old Fairlane (I affectionately called it "the boat," because the suspension was so bad that it leaned like a boat when I turned a corner), I would slump down just a bit so people wouldn't see who was driving it. I was a pastor, you see, and pastors are supposed to model success (and what a trap that is). One day I was driving the Cadillac and feeling good, and I heard these words in my spirit, "Kerry, why do you feel better about yourself in the Cadillac than you do in the Ford?"

Knowing that God never asks a question because He doesn't know the answer, I knew He was giving me an attitude check. I knew the answer to His question. I felt better about myself in the Cadillac because I was looking to external symbols of success to validate my worth. It didn't take me long to repent, but it took a while to walk into a revelation of my sonship.

Think about that occasion when you're driving down the road and see someone in their luxury vehicle, and the thought rises in your mind, "I wonder if they are somebody special." The answer is, they definitely are someone special, but it is not because of what they drive. They are special because they were made in God's image. But the luxury car has nothing whatsoever to do with who they are. They may feel perfectly at home in the BMW but could afford to pay cash for a Bentley. They may also be unemployed, three months behind on payments and running from the repo man. And statistics tell us that most millionaires are driving older cars and living in the same house they lived in twenty-five years ago! So outward appearances are deceiving. What's more important is that you are just as special, no matter what you drive, because you belong to *Abba*.

The wonderful thing about a revelation of your sonship is that it frees you from the pressure to be someone you're not.

The wonderful thing about a revelation of your sonship is that it frees you from the pressure to be someone you're not, or to measure up to some else's standards. If you are a son/daughter of God, there is nothing else to prove. This is the "rest" of faith:

> *For indeed the gospel was preached to us as well as to them; but the word which they heard did not profit them, not being mixed with faith in those who heard it. For we who have believed do enter that rest, as He has said: "So I swore in My wrath, they shall not enter My rest,'" although the works were finished from the foundation of the world ... There remains therefore a rest for the people of God. For he who has entered His rest has himself also ceased from his works as God did from His.*
> Hebrews 4: 2-3, 9-10

The question of a son is, can you feel the same way in an older VW as you feel in a new Beamer? It's not what you're in, but Who is in you.

C) Position

Position, like the other "counterfeits", is not initially a bad thing. Position is authority and all authority is from God (Rom. 13:1). But again, Satan's mode of operation is to take those things that are God-given and twist them so that we look to a resource as if it were The Source.

God is the only Source. Everything else is resource.

We see in Genesis that God raised up Joseph as the second-in-command to Pharaoh in Egypt in order to work a mighty deliverance for the people of God. Joseph understood this because God had given him two dreams in his childhood to help him understand both the "what" and the "why" of what was going to happen to him. So he tells his distraught brothers, "You meant this for evil, but God meant it for good" (Gen. 50:20). God has ordained His sons and daughters to rule, to lead, to have authority. But Jesus told His disciples that the leadership of sons looks totally different than the leadership of orphans.

> *You know that the rulers of the Gentiles lord it over them, and those who are great exercise authority over them. Yet it shall not be so among you; but whoever desires to become great among you, let him be your servant. And whoever desires to be first among you, let him be your slave—just as the Son of Man did not come to be served, but to serve, and to give His life a ransom for many.*
> Matthew 20:25-28

Positional Leadership Provides a Regular Drip of "Feel Good"

Satan was in the very Mountain of God before he rebelled and was cast out; he thinks he knows how this leadership thing works, and it is the core of his own destruction. We wouldn't be surprised to know that Satan uses "position," a God-ordained calling in the affairs of humanity, as a counterfeit. Position is seductive because a leader can so easily believe his own press releases. People in positions of leadership receive higher dosages of the "feel good juices" that come with affirmation, approval, "yes sir," "you're the boss," "whatever you say, sir." Of course, leaders know that there's a whole other side of challenge and sacrifice that goes with this—but it's still addictive.

Positional Leadership Can Numb the Pain with Busyness

The allure is that I can climb to heights of accomplishment that will prove that what they said about me in school was wrong. We also try to achieve past the pain of loneliness, thinking that if we stay busy enough we won't know that we're hurting. I can kill two birds with one stone: prove my antagonists were wrong and anesthetize the pain of loneliness with busyness.

Positional Leadership Looks Good in a Performance Culture

The praise of men is a powerful drug. And this drug is not only legal but lauded. The brass ring of a workaholic is the prize from a performance-driven culture. "It may not be Father's voice," we say to ourselves, "but at least it's somebody's voice saying, 'You're doing good'." Lacking a revelation of sonship, the orphan will run around with the loose end of an emotional "IV" willing to hook it up to anybody or anything that will give some affirmation. We end up begging for someone to tell us something good about ourselves. Psychologist, Jeremy Sherman writes:

> We all know folks who don't know how to handle [the lack of affirmation]. They're insatiable. Like humming birds to nectar, they need an ego-stroke every 15 minutes. Some people get rich and famous to support their ego-stroke addiction. They spend extravagantly just to convince themselves of their high status. Some run big countries, or at least try. Many just run countries, communities and families into the ground. Feeding them ego-strokes is like feeding gorillas. It takes a lot to keep them in supply.[24]

Stevie Wonder was singing about ego when he sang, "Everybody's got a thing, but some don't know how to handle it; always reachin' out in vain, accepting the things not worth having ...."[25]

Orphans are conditioned to accept things not worth having. The orphan spirit creates leaches out of people who just run from one person to the next looking for somebody to tell them they are doing something right. Why do people yearn for affirmation? Because they're not hearing the Father's voice saying, "You are My beloved son/daughter. In you I am well pleased." So we work for positions so that people under us will have to tell us how good we're doing (of course, this is never the initial or conscious reason we take a position, but it may be the unconscious driver). It is a subtle drip, but the people on your payroll will tell you how smart you are, how good you look, and how great you have done.

So how does this sound in the thoughts of our minds? Sometimes it sounds like this, "If I could get that job, that position, everything will work out for me. My problems will be solved." But we take our orphan-self with us to the new position, and like wearing really dirty clothes, as soon as we show up, so does the smell.

D) Power

Henri Nouwen says, "When we have come to believe in the voices that call us worthless and unlovable, then success, popularity, and power are easily perceived as attractive solutions."[26]

That is, *we only feel the need to show that we're somebody special if we are not sure that we are.* Jesus carefully contrasted the distinction between Kingdom power that serves in humility and humanistic power that demands subjection (see Mark 10:42-43). The humanistic cliché asserts, "Anything you can conceive, you can achieve." It fits so nicely with the "American dream"—but it simply isn't the nature of God. God reveals Himself through weakness, brokenness and humility. He confounds the powerful, the mighty, and the wealthy with His need of nothing.

Power is a Drug to the Orphan

Power is a drug to the orphan. Why is this? Because God has shared elements of His own power with man and the orphan lie tells us that with enough self-effort we can be "king of the hill." Only Satan actually saw God and believed he could be as powerful as God. The rest of us are willing to settle for just being more powerful than those around us.

God challenges Job's ignorance with, "Where were you when I laid the foundations of the earth?" (Job 38:4). And Jesus tells of the wealthy landowner that gets intoxicated with his abundance of stuff:

> *So your barns are full and you build bigger barns. But if your soul is required of you tonight, then who will all of this belong to?*
> Luke 12:18-20, paraphrase

James tells the wealthy to weep and howl because of the miseries that are coming upon them (James 5:1), and it almost sounds blasphemous to our ears.

Consider the Power of Weakness

God doesn't think in terms of either/or—either wealthy or poor, strong or weak. Sonship is about letting the power of God flow through our weakness, rather than running from our weaknesses. It's a third option. Paul saw that by the indwelling Holy Spirit the power of Christ rests upon us when we are neither moved by weakness nor strength, but by immediate obedience to the Father.

> **The power of Christ rests upon us when we are neither moved by weakness nor strength, but by immediate obedience to the Father.**

Notice that these are the things that Jesus was tempted with in the wilderness; the lust of the eyes, the lust of the flesh, and the pride of life. But the goal of Satan's temptation was not about things, it was about Jesus's identity as the Son. Yes, every temptation, when it comes down to it, is about your identity in sonship. Satan's repetitive precursor was, "If You be the son of God show Your power by doing this miracle or that one." Satan's mode of operation is to kill, steal and destroy, but his real objective is to separate you from the Father's love.[27]

Whether it is passions of the flesh, possessions, position or power, all of these things lead to a life of oppression. Every day we wake up asking the basic question, "What do I have to do today to feel like I'm somebody? What do I have to achieve today to succeed? What do I have to accomplish today so that somebody will say I am approved?" If you doubt this, just survey your social media account today and see how many people are talking about how busy and how tired they are. Busyness is the North American badge of importance.

Orphans Make the Best Recruits

In the motion picture, SKYFALL, James Bond and the Director of MI5 ("M"), have to flee London for safety. Bond takes the Director out into the country to his childhood home. They arrive on the vast estate, get out of the car and look at the majestic landscape. In a moment of rare personal reach, "M" asks Bond to recount his story about his parents' untimely death, leaving him a young orphan. He curtly responds, "You know the story," (i.e. I don't need to tell it to you). After an awkward silence the Director says, *"Orphans make the best recruits."*

Spiritual orphans make the best recruits for Satan's ploys because the orphan doesn't feel the love of a father, doesn't know if he has an identity, a home, or an inheritance. He is an easy target for the father of lies. Once you know James Bond was an orphan you can understand why he treats women as objects, is addicted to expensive toys, lives on constant adrenaline rushes, and has no real relational connections at a personal level.

The Impulsiveness of the Orphan Spirit

If orphans are grasping for position, possessions, passion, or power to gain a sense of identity, then one of the chief characteristics is that

Orphans can't see the value of contentment because they have emotional holes that need to be filled. they can't look to the future. They can't trust that God can take the pains of today and turn them into something glorious for tomorrow. They cannot see that the Father is molding sonship through today's adversity in a way that will bring the peaceable fruits of righteousness.

If the inner script in your head tells you that you will never have enough, be enough, or do enough to be valuable, you will grasp for what you can get now. The possibility that the delay may mean worthlessness is more than the orphan heart can bear. Orphans have to have it today; they have to have it now. Orphans have a shortcut spirit, which may include running over people on the way to where they are going. They have to assuage the feelings of "not good enough." It may mean moving from place to place to find a place of acceptance. It may mean buying clothes we don't need (retail therapy) to feel good about ourselves. It may seem as spiritual as acting on a prophetic word before praying and receiving godly counsel. It may mean going into debt in order to prove to others that you are "blessed." Orphans can't see the value of content because they have emotional holes that need to be filled. Even relationships become leveraged for what they can get out of it.

Someone said the marriage of two orphan-minded people is like two ticks and no dog; the ticks are sucking the life out of each other. No one is giving anything, but getting everything they can from each other until they both dry up and die. The parent-child relationship is the same. Orphan parents use their kids to provide for their own emotional fulfillment or therapy. It may sound absurd, but it's amazing to see how many parents are venting their anger, resentment and anguish on their children, because their children are the only ones that have to listen. They get their therapy from their kids, and what do you suppose that produces in those children?

Truth (facts) and knowledge is valued over love and life. The fruit of the Tree of the Knowledge of Good and Evil is valued above the fruit of the Tree of Life. Living from knowledge of good and evil, and acting out of that misplaced trust is more important than living from the Tree of Life: valuing relationships, forgiveness, transparency and openness.

Important Contrasts

Think about the contrast:
- An orphan fights to be right; a son would rather be rightly-related.
- An orphan has to state the facts; the son has to declare his love.
- The orphan has a right to know; the son will know what he needs to know when he needs to know it (because the Holy Spirit lives within him).
- Orphans rationalize why they have a right to say whatever they want to say; the spirit of sonship is going to cover with love.
- The orphan spirit says, "It's my duty to tell the truth even if it hurts someone; the spirit of sonship says, "There are things I know about you that I'll never repeat." So we commit ourselves to one another in love.

The Heavenly Father has better things in mind for you than to wear yourself out trying to prove who you are, or that you can. He has already secured your identity in His Son, and He loves you with the same love and in the same way He loves Jesus (John 17:23). We can wake up like a son, and the Holy Spirit is awakening you right now. He is stirring in you the appreciation of a new day to climb into Father's lap and feel His heart, find what His mission is, do whatever He tells you to do, and feel the joy of hearing His voice.

In the Father's perfect love you have:

Nothing to fear, nothing to prove, nothing to hide, and nothing to lose.

*Orphans run **from** the Father in fear. Sons and daughters run **to** the Father in unconditional love.* Go running into Father's arms. Recognize that the mission the Father gave Jesus was not to get the world "right", but to get the world reconciled to Himself. God was in Christ, reconciling the world to Himself (2 Cor. 5:19-20). Ben Campbell Johnson's paraphrase says:

God was in Christ, hugging the world to Himself. He no longer keeps track of men's sins, and has planted in us His concern for getting together.
2 Cor 5:19, Johnson

Orphans run from the Father in fear. Sons and daughters run to the Father in unconditional love.

What Have We Said?

We are made in God's image as relational beings, designed to live in overflowing fullness.

Satan's end-game is to offer various versions of "fake fullness" in an effort to ultimately separate us from the Father's love (and thwart the Father's loving purpose).

Orphans will settle for fullness substitutes: passions, possessions, position, and/or power. Each of these intoxicates like a drug.

Every temptation we will ever face will play on a God-given drive, thus easily rationalized, and is aimed at our identity—to get us to doubt our sonship.

Sons live in the fullness of the Father's love and know that the power of Christ rests upon us when we are neither moved by weakness or strength, but by immediate obedience to the Father.

Sons carry an awareness of an eternal future, which protects them from the impulsiveness of the now.

PRAYER

Abba, my addictions' gravitation pull toward "fake-fullness" only reveal that I am not really trusting You or understanding how You really see me. I want to run to You, Father, knowing that You will immediately begin to run to me. But the lies seem real, and it seems my entire life has been an evidence that the lies are true. I am asking You to remove the veil from my eyes. Come Holy Spirit. Speak truth in my spirit. Fill me with the fullness of God (Col 2:9-10; 3:19). Amen.

GROUP DISCUSSION

1. What are some verses of Scripture that reveal that we were made for fullness?

2. What is Satan's primary target in his business of temptation? Is it more than sinning?

3. What example can you think of in your own life where passions, possessions, position, or power have been a substitute for real fullness in God?

4. How would your life be different if you were totally unafraid of what others thought about you, or you had nothing to prove to anyone?

Eight

Transformation:
Turned into Another Man

Something majestic has to happen in our life
if we are to represent Jesus in His fullness.

As we learned from the progression of the orphan spirit, the enemy's end goal is to get you to believe you are all alone and on your own. Satan wants you to believe that God has left you, and left it up to you to make something of yourself. "You're going to have to do it yourself. Nobody is going to do it for you." Where does that come from? It comes from the father of lies that blinds our eyes to our identity in God and God's true nature of love toward us. Success, popularity, and power are easily perceived as attractive solutions to real fullness. An orphan will spend his life on the counterfeit—whether passions, possessions, positions or power—trying to dull the pain of "empty calories" and to prove who he is and that he has a home. It's the orphan theme song and The Rolling Stones made millions of dollars singing it, "I can't get no satisfaction …."

But a Son came on the scene and said, "My Father knows everything you have need of. And if you seek first His kingdom and His righteousness, all these things will be added to you." The glorious good news is that there is a Father who loves us and will take care of us perfectly. He wants you to be full. He has made a way for you to be full and have need of nothing.

Ponder This

Paul's prayer for the church at Ephesus (and for us), is a prayer that we might know experientially the Father's love and fullness. But he doesn't pray that we be filled with mere head knowledge, but with God Himself:

And I pray that you, firmly fixed in love yourselves, may be able to grasp (with all Christians) how wide and deep and long and high is the love of Christ—and to know for yourselves that love so far

beyond our comprehension. May you be filled
through all your being with God himself!

Ephesians 3:18-19 (J. B. Phillips)

Sons Rule by Revelation

We have gazed at length into the dark side of the battle; how humanity has been lured away from the perfect love of the Father by isolation, lies, counterfeit affections, and fake fullness. It's time to flip the script and see how the Holy Spirit redeems us out of "the bondage again to fear" (Rom. 8:15), and brings us to the powerful awakening that "Now we are the sons of God" (1 John 3:1-3).

In Chapter 1, I made a case for an experiential transformation: that the same way the enemy uses traumatic experiences, disappointments, and wounds as entry points to build a stronghold into our thinking, the Holy Spirit draws us into divine encounters, powerful experiences in the presence of God to replace the lies with Truth. No, the Holy Spirit would not be copying the ways of the enemy—Satan is the counterfeiter and has learned that God works by dynamic personal encounters. Consider the evidence: the Bible is full of the stories of men and women being transformed because God shows up, speaks a word, sends an angel, or gives a dream or vision. They have an experience with the Living God.

Transformation by Revelation

Here is a key to understanding how transformation works:

Humans are made in the image of God as spirit beings wired for relationship. Among other things, this means we live dynamically in experience, not just processing information cognitively. Part of the result of man's fall in sin was that his heart was darkened, he became spiritually dead (Eph. 2:1-2), which means he had to resort to living his life out of his mind instead of his spirit. But information is **Information is not transformation and never will be.** not transformation and never will be.

Information alone cannot transform anyone. If that were the case, the most educated would always be the most whole and transformed— and we know that's not true.

God's Spirit is working to release you from the tyranny of sadness, self-importance, and self-accusation.

Revelation by the Spirit is what transforms. This is so fundamental that Jesus declared the Church would be built upon the rock of spiritual revelation in the heart of man— and that revelation is that Jesus Christ is the Son of God (Matt. 16:16-18). Satan has only discovered by observation that humans are transformed by personal experiences, not just cognitive learning or reasoning. It is personal experiences, both good and bad, that trigger our belief system, release chemicals into the bloodstream and lock in a perceived truth into every part of a man's being spirit, soul and body. Whether man-made or demonically inspired, Satan opportunistically uses traumatic events or fears brought on by our experiences as a Trojan horse.[28] He is not that creative. Your personal history with God is the engine of transformation.

Isn't it interesting that the more cerebral the Church becomes the less powerful She is to deal with the spiritual needs of our world? Biblical training is more accessible than ever in history (books, videos, classes, etc.) and yet information alone doesn't transform. Is it a coincidence that Satan doesn't mind you going to church and hearing a well-planned, well-structured message, as long as you don't experience the presence of God with power? Is it a coincidence that, generally speaking, we are more comfortable with something we can control—talking about God—rather than something we cannot control—an experience with God?

Watch closely as the biblical narrative describes how transformation comes. We can see it clearly in the archetypal story of Saul, chosen of God to be the first king of Israel. He is living a non-descript, fairly purposeless existence until he has a personal encounter with Samuel, the prophet of God. In this story Samuel serves as a type of the Holy Spirit who pours oil over Saul's unsuspecting head to anoint him as king. Watch for the experience with the Spirit.

This Old Testament story foreshadows the importance of *The Abba Factor*. In it you will see how God's Spirit is working to release you from *the tyranny of sadness, self-importance,* and *self-accusation* that will keep you from rising to your true identity and fulfilling God's call to rule as a son or daughter of God here and now.

Kerry Wood

Saul: Training to Rule as a King

This is a story of your journey (and mine) into the transformation of sonship. The journey is mapped out for us in the story of Saul, son of Kish, anointed and called out of obscurity into kingly rulership—similar in so many ways to our own journey from orphans to sons. You can find this story in 1 Samuel, chapters 10 and 11. Note the significant statement that clues us to our common journey. Samuel, the prophet, the symbol of the works and word of the Lord, pours a flask of oil over Saul's head saying:

Is it not because the Lord has anointed you captain
over the Lord's inheritance?

1 Samuel 10:1

The background of this story, the selection and coronation of Israel's first king, begins with a man whom God sees as king, but the man is oblivious to God's good plan. In fact, Saul comes on the scene of history looking more like Jethro Bodine of *The Beverly Hillbillies*, or Lil' Abner, or Gastón of *Beauty and the Beast*, than an up-and-coming ruler. He's the larger-than-average country bumpkin who's been kicking around on his father's farm all his young life, without much initiative as to what life is all about. His grand introduction to history finds him on a fairly meaningless search for his father's lost donkeys. Not necessarily an ignoble pursuit, but possibly not even that meaningful considering Kish's small estate.

We must not miss the significance that Kish, Saul's father, represents one of the smallest families of the smallest tribe of Israel. Everything of his lineage and background spells "insignificant." But God is going to show His people—who want a king instead of the voice of God—what He can do with little or much.

The son and the father's servant pass through five different territories looking for these donkeys and Saul finally says:

Come, let us return, lest my father cease caring about the donkeys
and becomes worried about us.

1 Samuel 9:5

It is difficult for the reader to miss the fact that Saul doesn't perceive himself as any more important to his father than one of the servants.

But the servant accompanying him, a type of the Holy Spirit, not only watches out for, helps and cares for the unaware son, but gives him timely counsel on next steps. For when Saul is about to give up on the search, the servant points to the man of God.

> *Look now, there is in this city a man of God (a seer, prophet),*
> *and all that he says comes to pass. Let's go there,*
> *perhaps he can show us the way to go.*
>
> 1 Samuel 9:6

Before Saul and the servant enter the town, God has spoken to Samuel in preparation for the encounter. Samuel, who has been hearing from God since he was a boy in Eli's Shiloh Temple, arranges for the initiation of Saul's anointing. Samuel meets with Saul having set aside a large portion of meat for Saul. Listen to these words—they are significant to every son's journey to transformation. Samuel said:

> *Here it is, what was set back (set aside) for you. Eat,*
> *for until this time it has been set aside for you.*
>
> 1 Samuel 9:24

Every son must have a revelation that God has set something aside just for him. God has an inheritance for you with your name on it. There is a calling for you, a path for you, an inheritance for you. You are not wondering aimlessly through foreign territories hoping you stumble across your golden ticket to success. If you simply open your heart to Him, the Holy Spirit connects you to the word of the Lord which begins to reveal who you are and what is yours. You were born to be a king, and you have a territory that is yours.

Of course, just as we do, Saul immediately begins to protest the possibilities. He replays the script that has been running in his head all his life:

> *Am I not just a Benjamite, of the smallest of*
> *tribes of Israel, and my family the least of all the*
> *families of the tribe of Benjamin? Why do you*
> *speak like this to me?*
>
> 1 Samuel 9:21

Every son must have a revelation that God has set something aside just for him.

Samuel announces to Saul that they will meet the next morning. As Samuel (symbol of the working of the Holy Spirit) pours the anointing oil over the head of the unsuspecting, unaware son, he interprets the significance of the event for Saul saying:

> *Is it not because the Lord has anointed you captain*
> *over the Lord's inheritance?*
>
> 1 Samuel 10:1

By the way, the Holy Spirit wants to interpret the events of your life for you as well so that you don't miss what God is up to:

> *He will lead and guide you into all truth.*
>
> John 16:13

Transformational Checkpoints

Samuel then gives Saul careful instructions of five transformational checkpoints he must encounter. (Anointing to rule does not mean one is ready to rule). In digest form, what we see in these instructions is a customized deliverance process of Saul's own personal strongholds and re-programming of his mindset from orphan to son. What you will see in this process is a picture of how the Holy Spirit brings willing believers to personal transformation.

> *When you have departed from me today, you will find two men by Rachel's tomb in the territory of Benjamin at Zelzah .... Then you shall go on forward from there and come to the terebinth tree of Tabor. There three men going up to God at Bethel will meet you, one carrying three young goats, another carrying three loaves of bread, and another carrying a skin of wine. And they will greet you and give you two loaves of bread, which you shall receive from their hands. After that you shall come to the hill of God where the Philistine garrison is. And it will happen, when you have come there to the city, that you will meet a group of prophets coming down from the high place with a stringed instrument, a tambourine, a flute, and a harp before them; and they will be prophesying. Then the Spirit of the Lord*

110

will come upon you, and you will prophesy with them
and be turned into another man.

1 Samuel 10:2-6

What stands out to students of God's stories is that Saul has just been anointed by the prophet to be king, and is immediately enrolled in "Training for Reigning" boot camp. Saul has been chosen by God but still has nothing resembling a kingly mindset. He needs some divine experiences in order to rule effectively in the authority he has been given. Likewise, *every believer receives the anointing to rule by the indwelling Spirit, but must have encounters in God's presence that result in personal transformation. Salvation prepares us for heaven but does not automatically prepare sons of God to know how to "reign in life by one Christ Jesus"* (Rom. 5:17).

Steps to Ruling in God and Leading God's People:

1. Rachel's Sepulcher: Dealing with the emotional attachments of the past in order to move into your future.

Notice that the first place Saul is instructed to go is Rachel's Sepulcher at Zelzah. It's here that Saul will be challenged to focus on the future and forget the past—the lost donkeys have been found, now turn your attention to what's ahead. Rachel's tomb would have reminded every Hebrew of the intense sorrow that Jacob felt when he laid to rest the wife he loved so much. And at the same time the name, Zelzah means "clear shade" or "deceptive."

This may seem confusing, but note that there is a certain emotional severing we must experience by the power of the Spirit to leave our past behind. One might think that chasing lost donkeys for one's father would be an easy mission to abandon, and yet it is clear in the story that Saul was concerned about what his father would think if both the son and the donkeys didn't come home. But the deeper reality is that we get "hooked" on the business of non-productive endeavors. Think about our compulsions to constantly check our emails, social media, or stock market trends. Some old patterns must be broken if we are to rule and reign.

> **Every believer receives the anointing to rule by the indwelling Spirit, but must have encounters in God's presence that result in personal transformation.**

111

Hearing His voice and obeying what is heard. This is the first priority in transformation.

One of the first works of the Holy Spirit to prepare sons for Kingdom work is to deliver us from the deception of busyness, which has no eternal impact. Paul warns that our works, if not rooted in Kingdom purpose, will be burned up as wood, hay and stubble. There is a sadness that must be dealt with when we circumcise our hearts for God's purposes. Remember the rich young ruler that went away from Jesus's invitation with sadness? And how many men and women of God have you known that become tangled up in the cares of this world and never progressed past Rachel's Sepulcher? We respond to the voice of God and commit to Him, but then friends, jobs, identity markers, or habits keep drawing us back.

Paul tells young Timothy:

No one engaged in warfare entangles himself with the affairs of this life, that he may please him who enlisted him as a soldier.
2 Timothy 2:4

This would, of course, mean different things for different people because of our various giftings and callings. It is always dangerous to measure what "entangled" means based on someone else's calling and story. But for all of us, transformation begins with responding to a call to total commitment to the Lordship of Christ—which means hearing His voice and obeying what is heard. This is the first priority in transformation.

Let's stop and ask the Lord to speak about our own condition in this regard. Is there anything you keep going back to? Is there something you are emotionally connected to which has a hold on your affections? The Holy Spirit wants to release the *Abba Cry* in you concerning you and your anointing as a son. Do you want to talk to Him about that right now?

Selah—stop and think about this.

2. The terebinth tree at Tabor: The necessity of relational fellowship to stay grounded and clear-headed in the call.

The second station of Saul's process of "being turned into another man" was to go to the terebinth tree on The Plain of Tabor. There he would meet three men, one carrying three young goats (meat), one carrying three loaves of bread, and one carrying the wine.

Tabor means *"lofty"* or *"the heights."* Dear friend, do you know how the orphan heart responds to being called to be captain over God's inheritance? There are only two ways; either a spirit of rejection (to go hide) or a spirit of pride (to feel overly important). The "heights" could indicate to us that Saul would need some help to avoid getting "the big head." And how does Holy Spirit work that humility into our transformation?

Could it be that there are things in God that we cannot receive directly from heaven— but they must come through the hands of other believers in fellowship?

This story, given for our example, indicates that the best protection from getting too inflated about our newfound authority is in God-ordained fellowship. Saul is going to meet three other men who are headed to Bethel, "the house of God", to worship. Each man carried an important part of the worship... no, not guitars, Bibles and a sound system, but meat, bread and wine. These are always the symbols of intimate fellowship meals in the Scriptures. And we in North America struggle with this because extended intimate fellowship around a meal is almost unheard of in fast-food culture.

It is not my intent to interpret the story with point-by-point allegory, but it needs to be pointed out that Jesus's meat was to the do the will of the Father (John 4:34), He was and is the bread of life (John 6:35), and the new wine Jesus spoke of was a refreshing work of the Holy Spirit (Mark 2:22).

May I suggest that the next important work of transformation in the believer's life includes relationship among other believers who are "going up the hill of God to worship"? In the narrative, Saul is explicitly charged to "receive it (the elements of fellowship/worship) from their hands." *Could it be that there are things in God that we cannot receive directly from heaven—but they must come through the hands of other believers in fellowship?* Hebrews 6:12 says we are to "imitate those who through faith and patience inherit the promises." You have heard it said, some things are better caught than taught. And so, it is a humility forged by relationships that keeps us grounded in reality and truth.

Do you have strong relationships with people who are also "going up to God in worship"? Where are you when it comes to relationships in the kingdom? Do you think like the bumper sticker that said, "God, I love you; it's Your kids I can't stand"? Do you chafe under authority? Would you rather stay to yourself, "Go it alone"? Well, certainly you can do that, but the witness we have from Scripture is that your transformation happens in the context of relationality where we learn what it is to give ourselves away, sometimes without appreciation.

Lord, is there anything You want to say to me right now about opening my heart and life to those who are also "going up to the hill of God"? Would You help me find those brothers and sisters that would help me avoid "the heights" of ego and error? Selah.

3. The Garrison of the Philistines: Accepting your identity as a Kingdom man or woman, ready to withstand opposition and accusation.

The third boot camp assignment Saul was given was to go past the garrison of the Philistines at Gibeah. This is where the outpost of the occupying Philistines was stationed, and no doubt an intimidating experience. Think of these haughty, obnoxious Philistines who would take every opportunity to harass and intimidate the Israelites as they pass by that check point. Is that not a place you would want to avoid where possible? And yet, it was one of those check points located at an unavoidable place.

What happens after you have dealt with your sadness and reluctance about Rachel's sepulcher, and you have made the divine connections with friends going up the hill of God to worship? The Garrison of the Philistines represents the intimidation and accusation regarding your past, your qualifications, your gifts, and your own spirituality. In simplest terms, it is coming to grips with your new identity as a son of God. The Hebrew concept is called *Bar-Mitzvah* and it has to do with "coming of age in shouldering the responsibility of the Word"—being who you were called to be.

Every man and woman ever called by God has had to face the accuser of the brethren who launches crippling thoughts of unworthiness or slanderous words from others.

The truth is, *every man and woman ever called by God has had to face the accuser of the brethren who launches crippling thoughts of unworthiness or slanderous words from others.* For many men it is the harassing thought that "I'm not spiritual enough. I'm not as spiritual as my wife," or "I still have thoughts in my mind that aren't holy"—an attempt of the accuser of the brethren to get you to disqualify yourself. (By the way, don't confuse being religious with being spiritual. You are called to be a man or woman of the Spirit, not religious).

We feel the strong call of God upon our lives in a strong God-encounter—perhaps a worship service or an anointed message where God's Spirit is speaking to our heart—but in the solitude of the next day we have doubts as to whether we can really rise to this new place. For many women it may be all of this plus the thought that "there's no place where I can contribute." But rest assured my dear sister, that God does not give you gifts without opening doors of opportunity to minister those gifts to others.

This must have been a real problem for Saul because when the day of his coronation arrived and it was time for the people to put a crown on his head, he was nowhere to be found! They had to inquire of the Lord as to his whereabouts. Eventually they found Saul hiding out in the kitchen with all the food and supplies for the ceremony (1 Sam. 10:22). Now, *that* is an impressive leader; too intimidated to come to his own inauguration!

What is the *Abba* Factor and why is it important? It is God's Spirit working within you, crying "Abba, Father", that releases you from the **tyranny of sadness, self-importance,** and **self-accusation** that will keep you from rising to your true identity and fulfilling God's call to rule as a son or daughter of God here and now.

Will you be a man or woman of the Spirit? Will you allow the Holy Spirit to convince and convict you of your sonship, your authority, your Kingdom assignment? Do you have areas of intimidation where you naturally hide out in the kitchen, or where you automatically tell God that someone else could do it better? What does the Lord want to say to you about this right now? Perhaps you should write your thoughts in the margin and listen to His voice for a minute or two. Selah.

Just when you think boot camp is over …

There are two more significant encounters for Saul before he begins to reign as the first King of Israel.

4. Prophets Coming from the Worship: Stepping into Supernatural Ministry.

After Saul passes the intimidation of the Philistines he meets the Prophets coming down from the High Place. They have been in the presence of God; they have been worshipping and prophesying. This is supernatural ministry. This is life in the Spirit. But it speaks of more than a charismatic ecstatic experience. It also speaks of the shared leadership of a company or a team rather than the one-man icon so prevalent in our day. These prophets are prophesying, and the same spirit that is on them comes on Saul. When the Spirit comes on Saul two things happen—let's note them.

First, Saul begins to prophesy. Unless there are previous experiences the Scriptures don't tell us about, this is the first time Saul prophesies by the Spirit. He is learning to live and move in the supernatural.

Secondly, he takes his place among a company of supernatural people and "is turned into another man." This is the point, the goal, the objective of the Holy Spirit: to fill you with Himself to the point that your transformation is so evident that people will say you have been radically changed into a different person. It became so evident for Saul that people begin to take up a new song, "Is not also Saul among the prophets?"

Isn't that what you want? Isn't that really what we all want—to be turned into the kind of person by the power of the Spirit that fully represents Jesus for who He is? Yes, our education is good and needful. Yes, our character development is good and needful. Yes, our personality development is helpful. But all of that can be done to some degree by the power of the will. But Holy Spirit has been sent into your heart to do what you cannot do; to transform you from the inside out. *Let's ask Him to come and keep coming to us.*

Then there is the final station, which looks like anything but a celebration.

5. Gilgal: The cutting away of the flesh.

The final instruction the prophet gave Saul was to go down to Gilgal and meet the prophet there (1 Sam. 10:8). Why is this significant? Gilgal was the place where Abraham first went, he and his household, to be circumcised. This circumcision served as the sign of the covenant. Gilgal literally came to be known as the place of "the cutting away of the flesh," and many times Israel renewed its commitment to God at Gilgal. Paul picks up this theme for the New Testament believer as the Holy Spirit's work of sanctification:

And the father of circumcision to them who are not of the
circumcision only, but who also walk in the steps of that faith
of our father Abraham, which he had being yet uncircumcised.

Romans 4:12

For we are the circumcision, which worship God in the spirit,
and rejoice in Christ Jesus, and have no confidence in the flesh.

Philippians 3:3

And again:

In whom also ye are circumcised with the circumcision made without
hands, in putting off the body of the sins of the flesh
by the circumcision of Christ.

Colossians 2:11

This final work of the Spirit is not a one-time stop and go. Gilgal is a place that you and I return to again and again to re-affirm our submission to God and our rulership as sons of God. The Hebrew writer describes it as a training—"having your senses exercised to discern [the difference] between good and evil" (Heb. 5:14). It is the work of the Spirit to bring us back daily to declare that we put no confidence in the flesh, but our lives are an ongoing worship of God in the Spirit. It is also a place where we are to be set free from any nagging sense of unworthiness or sin-consciousness. *The Spirit of God wants to permanently seal your consciousness with sonship and divine favor.*

We Never Outgrow Sanctification

Do you know that as you get older the temptation is to put more and more trust in your experience and rely less and less on the Spirit of God to do a renewing work? It is our human tendency, as seen in the life of King Saul, David, Solomon and so many others, to do well in the beginning but to slowly put our confidence in our learning. As one wise pastor said, "The greatest danger with the ministry is that we can learn how to do it."

Can we be like the Apostle Paul, who in his older age said:

That I may know him, and the power of his
resurrection, and the fellowship of his sufferings,
being made conformable unto his death.

Philippians 3:10

The Spirit of God wants to permanently seal your consciousness with sonship and divine favor.

Unfortunately, King Saul will later fail at this point. He will make the mistake so many have made—to assume that familiarity with God buys some liberties with the flesh. But there are two anchors we should drop into our thinking here: we are anointed to rule by the Spirit, and to rule in the midst of our enemies (Ps. 110:2), but learning how to walk in that anointing is a process.

What Have We Said?

The Lord's purpose is to restore us to our place of sonship—as captains over the Lord's inheritance—the people God has chosen to be His inheritance.

The anointing oil immediately points to the role/work of the Holy Spirit in the transformation process. It's the Holy Spirit who transforms us into the Lord's purposes for us.

The anointing is followed by a series of transformational encounters prescribed to set our compass, calibrate our consciousness, to a life and destiny of reining as kings.

The *Abba* Factor is the Holy Spirit's releasing you from the tyranny of sadness, self-importance, and self-accusation that will keep you from fulfilling the Father's call to rule in the Son.

If, as I have asserted in Chapters 5 and 6, there is a progression toward an orphan spirit, wouldn't there also be a necessary progression into a spirit of sonship? If Saul's stations of preparation are any indicator, we should be progressing steadily toward a boldness to living as sons of God in the sunshine of the Father's favor.

So, what does transformation look like? I hope you are noticing that I have not given you a list of do's and don'ts and admonishments to try harder. The *Abba* Factor is about what the Holy Spirit is doing in you, synchronizing you (spirit, soul, and body)[29] to the image of the Father's Son.

PRAYER

> *Abba, I see how You knew exactly what Saul needed; each step of his transformation. It is encouraging to know that the Holy Spirit is leading me on a path for my full restoration from any lingering effects of the orphan spirit. Do You want to deal with pride in my life, inferiority or self-accusation, any regrets about my past? Holy Spirit, I trust You to speak to me at the right time—I submit to Your plan to train me as a son, to finish the Father's business with the Father's heart. Amen.*

In the following chapters we will look at the progression of the spirit of sonship.

GROUP DISCUSSION

1. What does Saul's anointing and journey to coronation tell you about the process of transformation to sonship (1 Samuel 10 and 11)?

2. What are the points of personal encounter Saul had to experience before he could rule as a king?

3. Which of these—the tyranny of sadness, self-importance, or self-accusation—are most like your own journey?

4. How are you positioned currently in the areas of God-ordained relationships in your life and presenting yourself regularly to the Lord for "the cutting away of the flesh" (sanctification)?

Nine

The Progression of the Spirit of Sonship

*May the God of peace ... make you complete (fully mature) in every
good work to do His will, working in you what is well pleasing
in His sight through Jesus Christ.*

Hebrews 13:20-21

We might anticipate that if there is a progression into the orphan spirit, there would also be a progression into a full awareness and lifestyle of sonship. And Paul's admonition to the Romans infers as much when he says:

*Do not be conformed to this world, but be transformed
(metamorphosed) by the renewing of your mind.*

Romans 12:2

In other words, there is a process involved in getting our thinking aligned to our new identity in order to walk out the will of God—which is our sonship.[30]

Saul's story (the previous chapter), with specific directions as to "next steps" (preparation to reign), symbolizes the Holy Spirit's orchestration of our progression into a realized sonship. Here's the brief review:

- Tyranny of Sadness—Dealing with Emotional Attachments of the Past
- Self-Importance—the heights.
- Self-Accusation—Gibeah and the garrison of the Philistines.
- Going Up the Hill of God—Engaging Relational Fellowship to Stay Grounded.
- Stepping into Supernatural Ministry—beginning to prophesy, and
- Ongoing Sanctification: The Cutting Away of the Flesh—Having our senses exercised to discern good from evil (Heb. 5:14)

Here is how the Holy Spirit begins to rebuild our identity as sons:

Twelve-Step Progression

1. Divinely Fulfilled Expectations: where our expectations are only in God.

The orphan spirit begins with failed expectations of those in authority. Sonship begins with a revelation of the awe, wonder, and faithfulness of God. To root out the fear that comes from broken promises and rejection from authorities, the Holy Spirit centers our focus on a series of promises and proceeds to reveal the Father as the Promise-keeping God (i.e. the covenant-keeping God), the God who declares Himself faithful, in whom there is not even a shadow of change (James 1:17). God puts His very existence on the line by making one promise after another to show that He is the only one who can be fully trusted.[31]

Please mark this down. Personal transformation never begins with who you are or what you do, but with who He is. It all begins with the infinite, overflowing love of God.

This volume couldn't contain a fraction of the promises of God that run like a thread, no … like a shipping rope, from beginning to end of the Scriptures. In fact, the Old Testament Scriptures were called "The Promises" (see Rom. 9:4; 15:8; 2 Cor. 7:1; Gal. 3:16). But here are a couple that cover the others:

My counsel will stand, and I will do all my pleasure,
Calling a ravenous bird from the east, the man that executes my
counsel from a far country: yes, I have spoken it, I will also bring it
to pass; I have purposed it, I will also do it.
Isaiah 46:10-11

Personal transformation never begins with who you are or what you do, but with who He is.

For all the promises of God in him are yea, and in him Amen, unto the glory of God by us.
2 Corinthians 1:20

Whereby are given unto us exceeding great and precious promises: that by these ye might be partakers of the divine nature.
2 Peter 1:4

And if God has invited us to know Him by giving and faithfully fulfilling every promise, what should our response be?

I will lift my eyes ABOVE the hills from whence comes my help. My
help comes from God, the maker of heaven and earth …
He shall not be moved.
Psalm 121:1-2[32]

Notice the Psalmist's eyes are not on his circumstances, or even the flaws of his authorities (though David had more than his share of opportunity to do so). His eyes were on God. When we keep our focus on ourselves and the failure of those around us depression comes. But begin to praise and worship the One who cannot fail us, and joy starts knocking on our door!

2. A Revelation that We Are Accepted in the Beloved.

If the next step into the orphan spirit is receiving our authority's failure as personal rejection, the path to a spirit of sonship would be a revelation that we are accepted in the Beloved, not rejected. Our dear friend, Wess Pinkham says, "In the Father there are no rejections—only redirections." The heart of that acceptance has nothing to do with our behavior or any personal quality that would meet some requirement. Our acceptance is rooted solely in the Father's love for His creation and the Son's willingness to become one with it through the incarnation.

Our failure to grasp the depth of this acceptance flows from a lack of understanding that in the incarnation, the Cosmic Christ who has been beside the Father since before time, was willing to commit Himself forever to the human cause by putting on humanity forever. As Trevor Hart says, "God has forever committed Himself to the human cause."[33]

This is how Jesus was "the Lamb slain from the foundation of the world" (before time) and is seen on the Throne right now as the Lamb bearing fresh marks of slaughter (Rev. 5:6). He has never put off humanity and is thus a High Priest who continues to be touched with the feelings of our infirmities (Heb. 4:15). When you and I see Him in Heaven we will still see the nail prints in His hands and side just as the disciples saw them in His resurrected body.

In fact, there is no reality to our being "in Christ" and "in the Spirit" if Christ's incarnation, His union with humanity, is not forever. It may seem heavily theological, but make no mistake—your acceptance in the Beloved is not secure because you are trying hard enough. It is vouchsafed—granted in graciousness—in the incarnation of the Son, "a Man sat down at the right hand of God" (Heb. 10:12).

All of this is made real to us by the Holy Spirit becoming a "spirit of wisdom and revelation" in our spirits. This is precisely Paul's prayer (Eph. 1:17-23), asking God to grant that work in the believers at Ephesus. He prays that we would come to know in our spirit the following:

- The hope of His calling,
- That we, the saints, are the glorious inheritance He has chosen for Himself,
- And the exceeding greatness of the power that is at work in us by the indwelling Holy Spirit.

All of these God released in us through Christ when He raised Him from the dead and seated Him at the highest place of authority.

In this, God is birthing in you an understanding that you are already accepted and loved. We do not have to fight for acceptance. Just like we are born with certain physical traits; when we are born again, God's acceptance of us already comes pre-attached. It's a package deal! The Holy Spirit is convicting and convincing you of this current reality, not trying to make it happen.

3. Restored Trust Experienced in The Power to Forgive.

We have seen that Satan uses our sense of rejection from our parents' imperfections to destroy our sense of trust in others. What does the Holy Spirit do through the *Abba Cry*? He leads us back into trust, first by coming to know God as the trustworthy One who keeps His promises, and secondly by leading us into powerful experiences of forgiveness.

Since we have already touched on the "promise factor," let's look at how being freely forgiven enables us to freely forgive.

Freely you have received, so freely give.
Matthew 10:8

We can draw on the freely-given strength of the Spirit to forgive others. This comes directly from the grace we have received in our own forgiveness. People who haven't received forgiveness find it very difficult to forgive others (because it is not a natural, but supernatural work). Hurt people hurt people, broken people break people, forgiven people forgive people. Trust is a work of the Spirit, and our partnership is to forgive and bless. I learned this the hard way.

When you step out and bless those who have wounded you, the Holy Spirit heals your emotions and simultaneously rebuilds a trust-capacity in you as a son of God.

The Hard Lesson of Double-Barrel Forgiveness

I was a senior pastor at the ripe old age of twenty-five (keep praying for those poor folks). An older gentleman in that fifty-year old church said some very critical things about me publicly (most of them deserved, I'm sure). A few days later the severity of his accusations began to settle in on me and I felt a wall of bitterness rise up within me. The Lord began to show me the double-barrel work of forgiveness and inner healing. The first step was to choose to forgive and release. I had done that: "Father, I release him. I forgive him. I do not hold these words against him and ask You to forgive him" (John 20:23). However, it was more difficult to pull the trigger on the second "barrel."

The second part of forgiveness is not so much about the offender, but more about the offended person's own healing. Jesus spoke to my heart quoting Luke 6:28:

Bless those who curse you; pray for those who despitefully use you.

I instinctively knew that He was telling me that the only way to be healed in my emotions from this wound would be to pro-actively pray for and bless this man. I knew I could, because so many blessed me in the same way.

This is a powerful factor in the rebuilding of trust as a necessary step in the progression of your sonship consciousness. *When you step out and bless those who have wounded you, the Holy Spirit heals your emotions and simultaneously rebuilds a trust-capacity in you as a son of God.* Many believers get stuck right here. I have seen young and old believers alike that have

There is no single facet of our new life in God that has more impact upon the transformation from orphan to son than hearing the Father's voice for ourselves.

stalled in their spiritual growth, and upon deeper investigation, they refused to pray for and bless someone who had wounded them. They bought into the lie that "I may have to love them, but I don't have to like them." Usually without admitting it, they would settle for being absent from each other forever rather than to humble themselves and be reconciled. Unforgiveness is a killer in the body of Christ.

4. A Spirit of Faith that comes through the spoken, experiential hearing of the Word of God.

There is no single facet of our new life in God that has more impact upon the transformation from orphan to son than hearing the Father's voice for ourselves.

Satan plays on our childhood experiences of perceived abandonment and lack to imbed a spirit of fear, but the Holy Spirit replaces that fear with a bold faith that comes from hearing the voice of God in your own spirit. And where do you think Satan got the idea that he could ensnare people's souls (mind, will and emotions) by using traumatic experiences as entry points except that he watched the transformational encounters take place when God spoke to men?

Paul tells the believers at Rome that faith is not something you muster up or even pray for—it is the byproduct of hearing God's voice in your spirit:

Faith comes by hearing, and hearing (this kind of hearing—hearing in your spirit) comes by the word (rhema) *of God.*
Romans 10:17

This sounds extremely simplistic, but when God speaks, His words create. He is not giving suggestions, He is creating faith in our hearts with words that contain self-reproducing power for fulfillment.

When the Father spoke from heaven at Jesus's baptism at Jordan, *"This is my beloved Son in Whom I am well pleased,"* He was injecting a sonship consciousness in Jesus that would sustain Him through the upcoming wilderness temptations. More than good counseling, more than another seminar, more than "Six Steps to Success," you need a word from God.

In my own life, I can take you to at least a dozen places where I have had life-altering encounters with God by hearing His voice. (It is actually a powerful exercise to think back over your own personal journey and list all the times and locations where you "met God"). At the very lowest point in my life, the Father spoke in my spirit by the Holy Spirit saying, "Kerry, if you'll make Me (the Holy Spirit) your best friend, you'll have what you need to have when you need to have it, and you'll know what you need to know when you need to know it."

That word (and many others) created a faith for provision in me in that hour that has never faded. God's voice, Spirit to spirit, is what creates faith in us and replaces the fear that returns us again and again to bondage (Rom. 8:15). But He doesn't just speak to answer your questions or to give you a bit of information—He speaks to transform you and to put a sword in your hand for action.

This is a key landmark in your progression into sonship—you have heard the Father's voice (perhaps a whisper, an internal witness, a picture or one of the many ways He speaks), and you have taken that word up as your sword and shield—using His word to deflect all the fiery darts of the orphan spirit.

> *... and taking the shield of faith with which you will be able to quench all the fiery darts of the wicked one ... and the sword of the Spirit, which is the Word (rhema, spoken) of God.*
>
> Ephesians 6:16-17

Has the word that God has spoken to you become an offensive weapon against Satan's lies—a sword in your mouth? Are you engaging in the battle with that word?

5. The Vulnerability of a totally, trusting, secure son.

Watch carefully how the Holy Spirit weaves a seamless tapestry of redemptive transformation in the inner working of the spoken Word, to learning trust in that word, then to an inter-dependent spirit (numbers 4, 5 and 6 of the progression of sons). We can see it so clearly in Hebrews 13:5-6:

> *For **He Himself (the Lord) has said,** "I will never leave you nor forsake you,"So that we may boldy say:"The Lord is my helper; I will not fear. What can man do to me?*

God speaks to us as His sons and says, *"I will never leave you nor forsake you—I am with you and I am for you."* That word creates a new faith in us. It speaks sonship in us. It reformats the hard-drive of our broken trust, insecurity, sense of abandonment and fear. That spirit of faith empowers me to speak (2 Cor. 4:13) so that I begin boldly saying what He has said to me, *"The Lord is my Helper. I will not fear. What can man do to me!"*

The orphan spirit relied on self-protection because our spirit was closed to others. Self-protection is an orphan skill. But Jesus, as the perfect Son, committed His protection into the hands of His Father. He drew a sense of fullness and identity from another place. The heavens had opened, and the Spirit was given Him without measure. He was full of the infinite God and therefore could give himself away freely. Giving himself away daily wasn't a deity trick. Laying His life down and living the "form of a servant" wasn't something He only did on the cross when He said, *"Father, into Your hands I commit my spirit."* He had been doing that every day by the power of the Holy Spirit. He only spoke what He heard the Father saying. He only did what He saw the Father doing. He did all of this by yielding, trusting totally in the indwelling Spirit.

The sweat drops of blood in Gethsemane were not the result of Jesus working really hard to do the right thing. This was the greatest sign of a totally trusting, secure son who knew His Father was with Him and for Him. He was living by the Word of His Father; eating a bread that His disciples didn't know about yet. Yes, on the cross His soul (emotions) felt it to the core, venting the cry, *"Why have you forsaken me?"* But He (His spirit, by the Holy Spirit), never doubted—*"Father, into your hands I commit my spirit."*

You and I are called to a place of Spirit-fullness where the voice of the Father is ringing within us, and the love of God is so shed abroad in our hearts by the Holy Spirit (Rom 5:5), that we are empowered to open ourselves to the risk of being hurt again. We commit our very existence into God's hands and find a place by the Father where there is nothing to fear, nothing to prove, nothing to hide, and nothing to lose.

"I have said … so that you may boldly say … "

6. From an independent spirit to an inter-dependent spirit.

The orphan spirit is an independent, self-reliant attitude. But the spirit of sonship is an interdependent, relational spirit. The more you and I are drawn into the life of the Father, Son, and Spirit by the *Abba Cry*, the more we understand we were never meant to be alone or to try to succeed on our own. Remember, Saul was instructed to meet the group of worshipers coming down from the hill of God—

The spirit of sonship is an interdependent, relational spirit.

engaging in relational fellowship to stay grounded—and perhaps this step provides insights into Saul's later failure as a king. It's easy to buy into a notion of individualism when you've been anointed as a king. But God rules in Triune relationship—and we must rule in relationship as well.

The Spirit is given individually; but for the purpose of working us into the community. Our spirit only remains closed where there is a lack of trust, a lack of faith, a lack of love of God, a lack of personal healing in our own soul, a rejection of the grace of God. Unforgiveness keeps my spirit closed to others. We don't want to talk to someone or be with someone if we have unforgiveness toward them. But when I'm full of the Spirit, everyone looks better to me, the world is beautiful to me, and we love being with others. God is a relational being, and being full of God leads us to healthy relationality. The more individualistic we become the farther we are from God.

Paul's great metaphor of the Body drives a stake through the heart of isolation and independence. He plainly states that:

> *The hand cannot say to the eye, I don't need you.*
> 1 Corinthians 12:21

You have been baptized into a living community of Father, Son, Holy Spirit—that is, all those who are in that Triune relationship by virtue of being in Christ. Neither you nor I have the option of living with unforgiveness or isolating ourselves from other members of the Body.

Jesus says:

> *Don't bother bringing your worship to God until you get those kinks worked out* (as best as you can) *between you and your brother.*
> Matthew 5:24, my paraphrase

John says:

> *How can you say you love God whom you have not seen if you don't love your brother that you do see?*
> 1 John 4:20

What Have We Said?

The first part of the progression from orphan to son looks something like this:

1. Divinely Fulfilled Expectations: where our expectations are only in God.
2. A Revelation that we are accepted in the Beloved.
3. A restoration of trust experienced in the power to forgive. This forgiveness includes "a double-barrel" work of choosing to forgive and learning to pro-actively pray and bless those we are forgiving.
4. A Spirit of Faith that comes through the spoken, experiential hearing of the Word of God.
5. A restoration of vulnerability in trust and security.
6. Transformation from an independent, self-reliant individual to one who is giving and receiving in community.

PRAYER

Abba, You have declared my deliverance from orphan thinking and my transformation into sonship. You have said all You have said, so that I may boldly say the same. I agree with You. I agree that I am the righteousness of God in Christ. I agree that I have been transferred from the kingdom of darkness to the kingdom of Your unconditional love. I agree and boldly declare that I am now a son of the Most-High God, and am beginning to enjoy the inheritance of that sonship through Jesus Christ, by the indwelling Holy Spirit. Thank You for continuing to transform me from glory to glory by the Spirit of the Lord. Amen.

GROUP DISCUSSION

1. What does Hebrews 13:5-6 tell us about our role in the process of transformation?

2. What are the two facets of forgiveness ("the double barrel") necessary for emotional and spiritual healing?

3. Which of these six steps toward sonship seem to be the most difficult step for you?

Ten

The Progression of the Spirit of Sonship Continued

Sonship is not forcing but feasting,
not performance but presence.

Before we conclude the progression of sonship we should note that neither the progression of the orphan spirit nor of sonship is necessarily sequential in all cases. It is apparent that there are connections spiritually and psychologically. I am not suggesting that the Holy Spirit takes every person down the same path in order to restore in us a sense of our sonship. Sonship is not a destiny to which one arrives nor a grade that one achieves. You don't try to "get it", you invite His presence; He comes to you. Sonship is a relationship in God that is strengthened by life in the Holy Spirit, the Spirit of Adoption. But the nature of humanity's brokenness is universal in many ways, and so can be the cure.

In the previous chapter we established the rebuilding of fulfilled expectation, acceptance in the Beloved, restoration of trust with the power to forgive, a renewed spirit of faith, the power of vulnerability and security, and development of an inter-dependent and relational way of being.

This inter-dependent, relational way of being is expressed in honor. This is the next step in the progression of the spirit of sonship.

Twelve-Step Progression Continued

7. Honoring others in their gifts, callings and differences.

The orphan spirit only knows to control and manipulate relationships, but a spirit of sonship is un-controlling and honoring. The world doesn't understand this and even defines leadership as the ability to get others to do what one wants them to do. Many of our organizational rules are created out of fear of repeating problems or

A spirit of sonship is un-controlling and honoring.

unmanageable people and circumstances. The goal is uniform behavior and thinking. A pastor friend of mine says, "rules are made so elders can sleep at night." Our churches and organizations are either rules-oriented or relationship-oriented; high rules equal low relationships, and low-rules equal high relationships. Uniformity sacrifices individual creativity. Where there is a high value on deep relationships, there will be honor and value placed on each person's gifts, callings and differences.

God is Secure and Uncontrolling in His Own Being

Consider how un-controlling our loving God is. He made humanity and delegated the authority and responsibility to humans to have dominion over the whole planet, and watched as Adam and Eve abdicated that authority to the conniving usurper that God had kicked out of heaven.

Consider how uncontrolling God is that He would honor humankind's free will (His image in humanity) to let us turn the keys of the planet over to Satan, or even to let us walk away from Him. We don't understand how He can be so secure that He allows us to rage against Him, curse Him with clinched fist, without being intimidated at all. He has no emotional holes to fill. His is full, fully loving and other-centered. He has no capacity for insecurity. But brokenness and insecurity in humans wants to control others, minimize dialogue, and threaten those that believe differently.

Sons are Secure and Uncontrolling

As the Holy Spirit convinces you of your own sonship, secured in the relationship between the Father and Son, you become more composed, more at rest in your own spirit. Like Father, like son—you discover that you don't have to defend God or His truth—He is not even defending Himself. He is quite happy to celebrate the diversity of His own multi-faceted nature as revealed in humanity. He is more interested in being rightly-related than being "right." Sons are relaxed, not threatened around diversities of opinion. The more convinced you are in who you are, the less anxious you are about those who think differently.

The more convinced you are in who you are, the less anxious you are about those who think differently.

Listen to the calm voice of Jesus as He responds to the Roman governor's inquisition:

"Don't you know that I have the power to spare your life
or take it from you?" And Jesus calmly says,
"You have no power except what is given to you by my Father."
John 19:10-11, my paraphrase

The officials were perplexed that Jesus didn't try to defend Himself —"as a lamb before the slaughter, He opened not His mouth." He had nothing to hide, nothing to lose, nothing to fear, and nothing to prove. He was secure in His Father's love … and we can be too.

Can you trust the Holy Spirit? Can you allow others to be at a different place in God than you? Can you be as sure about the Holy Spirit's ability to bring others to spiritual maturity as you are of your own? We are all growing in God, not because some of us are better at it than others, but because the Holy Spirit is tenacious.

The One who is faithful to call you, (He) *also will perform it.*
1 Thessalonians 5:24

8. Relational Intimacy Experienced in Fellowship (*Koinonia*).

Where the orphan spirit settles for superficial relationships, a spirit of sonship experiences intimacy in giving and receiving. In the New Testament, this is seen in the fellowship (*koinonia*) of the Early Church. One of the most counter-cultural marks of the Early Church was their uncommon love for one another. Luke tells us these believers did life together and were filled with generosity:

Now the multitude of those who believed were of one heart and one
soul; neither did anyone say that any of the things he possessed was
his own, but they had all things in common.
Acts 4:32

The cry in every human soul is for deep, intimate knowing in relationship. Our relational God hard-wired us to need to know and be known—for someone to know you "warts and all" and still completely love and accept you. This is what you were made for and what the Holy Spirit is doing—this is the *Abba* Factor. All of us are totally loved, totally accepted sons of the Father. As we become convinced of this in our spirit, we lose the

135

fear of not having enough, not doing enough, or not being enough. And we become free to be ourselves and to give ourselves away.

Having had the opportunity to serve both as a pastor and professor for some years, there have been numerous young men and women who have asked for "the secret" to successful ministry. I often share what the Holy Spirit shared with me years ago. He said it to me this way:

> **Know** who you are and what you have to give.
> **Value** who you are and what you have to give.
> Then **give** who you are and what you have to give,
> To those who will **receive** who you are and what you have to give.

Of course, the key to this is "by the Spirit." Only as we get full of the Spirit and stay full as sons in constant communion, can we know who we really are and what we have to give, and live in the security of sonship so as to give ourselves away freely. This leads us to the necessity of our Source of sonship.

9. Sons Receive Their Thoughts and Appetites from the Spirit.

One of the greatest benefits of the spirit of sonship is that the Holy Spirit is welcomed to transform the "want to's" of the believer from the orphan lies to an experiential fullness of life in God. This is not by bombarding the mind with "good" and "holy" thoughts, though that is certainly better than taking in bad and unholy ones. But it is an inside-out process whereby the indwelling Spirit "downloads" the will and purposes of God into your own spirit. The synchronization of your heart with God's is the focus of the sequel book, *The Abba Formation*, but suffice it to say that God has not left it up to you and me to come up with His thoughts on our own, nor has He dropped a big book out of the sky and left us to figure out what it says.

He has actually moved in—taken up residence inside of us in order to teach us, lead and guide us into all truth and show us things to come (see John 14 and 16). The lies that make us susceptible to passions, possessions, position and power are displaced, by the Spirit of Truth, with the awareness that in Christ I have "all things." But don't make the common Western mindset mistake that it is just about more knowledge in your head. Fullness of Him—not just knowledge per se—is the antidote to every temptation the enemy can throw at you.

Think about how difficult it would be for the enemy to tempt you if you were full, totally satisfied and in need of nothing in every area of your life. Do you know why you are never supposed to go to the grocery store when you're hungry? Because you will put everything you see in the grocery basket! And most of it won't be good for you. But if you are full, you won't be driven by hunger but by wisdom and strategic purpose.

Fullness in the spirit feels like a fire in your inner man.

The Holy Spirit keeps pointing to Jesus, and Jesus in turn fills us with His Spirit. It seems we want to find every "best practice," technique, and human innovation possible rather than simply do what Jesus did: get full and stay full of the Spirit. The more you and I stay full of the Spirit, the less room there is to be lured by alternatives.

10. Learning to live in the Overflowing Fullness of the Spirit.

Rather than accepting fake fullness, sons learn that they live by every word which is continually proceeding from the mouth of the Father (Matt. 4:4). His words are spirit (*pneuma*) and they are life (*zoe*), which is the very life of God Himself. As W.E. Vine says it, "life as God has it." We are to feed on Him, the Person, as our daily bread (John 6:38).

Do you think Jesus was just being snarky to say:

> *Unless you eat of my flesh and drink of my blood,*
> *you have no part in me?"*
>
> John 6:53

No, He was pointing to a personal and intimate relationship with Him as Person, not just precepts and principles that can be dissected analytically in the mind.

Fullness in the spirit feels like a fire in your inner man. Remember the men walking on the road to Emmaus, after spending time with Jesus they said:

> *Did not our hearts burn within us while He opened the Scriptures to us?*
> Luke 24:32

Can you see why a Christianity that is only emotional or logical leads to spiritual malnutrition and starvation?

Displacement of orphan lies, by the Spirit of fullness, is better than conquest by willpower. Humanity was designed to live full, love full, work full, and play full. The only reason we have had to develop sin management systems and religious programs of constraint is because we ignored the simple plan of God to fill us with Himself. The New Testament command is to be filled with the Spirit (Eph. 5:18). As far as Peter was concerned, the clear sign that Gentiles had been grafted in was the fullness of the Spirit (Acts 15:8). And Paul tells us the way to put the works of the flesh to death is "by the Spirit" (Rom. 8:13). And the only way to have a genuine passion for the lost and to see justice for the marginalized, is to stay full. Every other path becomes a political agenda.

The real freedom regarding our appetites is not that we get strong enough to master them, or to control every thought; but that we allow Him to displace our thoughts with His thoughts, by the Spirit (Phil. 2:12-13). It is the Spirit of Abba that

> ... creates and energizes in you both the will (the "want to") and power (the ability) to do His good pleasure.
> Philippians 2:13 (AMP)

Displacement of orphan lies, by the Spirit of fullness, is better than conquest by willpower. If you are struggling to master your spiritual journey by willpower, you have not yet discovered the secret to "the easy yoke." His yoke is easy because "it is not by might, nor by (human) power, but by the Spirit of the Lord." In the sequel *The Abba Formation*, we discuss how to get full and stay full of the Spirit in the chapter entitled "The Language of the Spirit of Sonship."

11. Sons Speak the Truth in Love and worship in Spirit and Truth.

The progressive development of the orphan spirit involves a life and language of self-deception. Orphans learn how to rationalize their bondage and call it freedom. Satan is a master at redefining terms; but the progression of the spirit of sonship is a progression into light and truth because sons embrace more transparency of heart and soul. Sons learn to confess their faults and live in the light. Sons come to realize that the only way Satan can hold them in bondage is if they keep something hidden in darkness; as soon as it is brought into the light it has no power. Sons learn to let their yes be yes and their no be no (communication without deception).

The One Another Gospel

The life of sonship is a life in the Trinitarian circle of affirmation and overflowing love. The Father is blessing the Son, the Son is blessing the Spirit, the Spirit is binding the Father and Son together in love, and the sons of God are drawn up into this life of blessing as the Holy Spirit empowers us to live out the fifty-eight "one-anothers" of the New Testament. We give ourselves away in love by admonishing one another, loving one another, bearing one another's burdens … and all of that is by the overflowing power of the Spirit. (For more, see *The Abba Foundation*.)

What is our worship, but a participation in that Triune circle of affirmation and love? The Father pours out strength, wisdom, blessing, honor, and glory upon His sons and daughters by the Spirit. In response we are filled with a reciprocating worship—and we sing:

> *Blessing, glory, honor, power, might, and dominion, be unto thee.*
>
> Revelation 4:11

The worship that the Apostle John saw going on in heaven two-thousand years ago is still happening right now as the family of God, both in heaven and earth, bless the Lord. This is what Jesus is referring to when He tells the Samaritan woman:

> *God is a spirit, and those that worship Him worship*
> *in spirit and in truth.*
>
> John 4:24

By the way, sons are not quiet, timid folk; they have been set free to praise God in a new way of living and being. Wherever you find people who are full of the Spirit, you will find spontaneous, uninhibited, grateful worship. It's a rather simple by-product of spiritual feasting and fullness.

12. Sons Live by the Power of the Spirit—The Triune Life of God.

Rather than living a life of oppression, sons of God are other-centered, generous, overflowing, and continually growing in grace (more and more freedom) and in the experiential knowledge of the Lord. Sons of God are being led by the Spirit of God (Rom. 8:14) to be about the Father's business. This means we have come to a place in God where we are not having to spend inordinate amounts of time trying to get ourselves fixed, though that process is never over in this lifetime. There is an abundance in God—an overflowing fullness of righteousness, peace and joy that comes by life in and with the Spirit, who continually confirms our sonship in us.

Please allow me to repeat something in order to give you an example of how the Holy Spirit confirms our sonship in us. I remember one day in prayer when the Lord spoke lovingly but forcefully to me. It was clearly a corrective word. I had been pastoring for almost thirty years, but continually striving for something else. One day I heard the Holy Spirit whisper in my spirit saying, "Kerry, quit trying to get yourself perfected and just start giving away what I have given to you." Out of that exchange He burned in my spirit what I shared earlier in this chapter.

Know who you are and what you have.
Believe in who you are and what you have.
Give who you are and what you have,
To those who will receive who you are and what you have.

The Holy Spirit has so much He wants to say to you. His words will fill you, change you, and re-format your hard drive. The more you give away, the more He will be speaking to you.

Life In Abundance

The orphan fear is that someone will not accept who I am or what I have, and it is true. If they rejected Jesus and what He had to offer, someone will surely reject you. But you don't need to live there. That is not your concern, because for all those who won't receive who you are and what you have, there are scores of others who are hungry and thirsty for what you bring to the table. Stay full of the Spirit, be led by the Spirit, and give yourself away. You will never lack anything you need.

It's the *Abba* Factor—the work of the Holy Spirit, convicting and convincing me of my sonship. It's not something I am trying to become—it is who I "be." Therefore, I cannot give away what I have in God that I don't turn around and find the pantry has been mysteriously re-stocked! I am in Him, He is in me, and He lacks nothing.

What Satan has broken and distorted in us in the orphan progression, the Holy Spirit restores through the *Abba Cry.*

Ponder This

Whatever we think the Holy Spirit is doing in us and in our world, it's bigger. Clark Pinnock broadens our horizons on the Spirit's work beautifully saying:

> *The Spirit reaches out to creatures, catches them up and brings them home to the love of God. Spirit is serendipitous power of creativity, which flings out a world in ecstasy and simulates within it an echo of the inner divine relationships, ever seeking to move God's plans forward .... The Spirit is bringing God's plans to completion in the direction of new creation and union with God through the participatory journey of Jesus Christ ... Spirit is the ecstasy that implements God's abundance and triggers the overflow of divine self-giving. In the Nicene Creed he is called the "Lord and giver of life."*[34]

What Have We Said?

The progressive work of the Spirit starts with resetting expectations and broken trust and ends with a fullness that propels sons and daughters to live in full freedom of the Father's blessing. What Satan has broken and distorted in us in the orphan progression, the Holy Spirit restores through the *Abba Cry.* It looks like this:

1. Divinely fulfilled expectations: where our expectations are only in God, to
2. A revelation that we are accepted in the beloved, to

3. Restored trust experienced in the power to forgive, to

5. A spirit of faith that comes through the spoken, experiential hearing of the Word of God, to

6. The vulnerability of a totally, trusting, secure son,

7. From an independent spirit to an inter-dependent spirit, to

8. Honoring others in their gifts, callings and differences, to

9. Relational Intimacy Experienced in Fellowship (*Koinonia*), to

10. Receiving Thoughts and Appetites from the Spirit, to

11. Learning to live in the overflow of Spirit Fullness, to

12. Speaking the Truth in love and worship in Spirit and Truth, to

13. Living by the power of the Spirit—The Triune Life of God.

Does it sound too good to be true? The reality is, Jesus came as a son to show us how we could live, here and now, by the indwelling Holy Spirit— and He lived this way among us. If it seems impossible to your mind, it is impossible for us, but not God. This is what the Holy Spirit is actively doing in those who will make space for Him to speak and work daily. The question remains—how do we cooperate with Him? We will finish strong by looking at how we move from orphans to heirs in our last chapter.

PRAYER

Abba, how can I express the depth of my gratitude for Your furious and infinite love! I say with Paul, "Oh, the depth of the riches both of the wisdom and knowledge of God! How unsearchable are Your judgments and Your ways past finding out! "For who has known Your mind? Or who has become Your counselor? Or who has first given to You and it shall be repaid to him? Thank You, Holy Spirit, that You are making these things known to us now as sons. For of Him and through Him and to Him are all things, to whom be glory forever. Amen.

GROUP DISCUSSION

1. Which of these twelve steps do you feel you have seen the most and least progress thus far?

2. Can you allow others to be at a different place in God than you?

3. Do you feel you are still trying to become something else, or do you sense God is showing you who you already are in Him?

4. To what degree do you feel you must defend God—fight for the "right?"

Eleven

From Orphans to Heirs

Our good Father will always give to you what He asks from you.
If you feel He is asking something of you that is not in your hand,
start looking around; it's close.

We need a starting point, some basic first steps to know we're on the right track without taking the burden upon our own shoulders to make this happen. A fundamental awareness of the nature of God is that He has everything and needs nothing. Therefore, He will never ask anything of you that He has not already given to you. Another way to say this is the way the Lord spoke it to me at a very low moment in my life, "Kerry, you will always have what you need to have when you need to have it." He will provide for me anything He is asking of me. Before I give you five steps to move from orphans to heirs, I want to take you back to a pivotal shift in God's redemptive history—in particular from Old Testament to New.

Restoration of Sonship

In Malachi 4, the last words of the old covenant give a hope and also an ominous challenge moving toward the new covenant:

Behold, I will send you Elijah the prophet before the coming of the
great and dreadful day of the LORD. And he will turn the hearts
of the fathers to the children, and the hearts of the children to their
fathers, lest he come and smite the earth with a curse.
Malachi 4:5-6

I've always read that passage and asked, why Elijah? And I would think about Elijah calling down fire on the prophets of Baal, and that spirit of revival and power, and assumed it was because we need that revival and that power in the new covenant. But that was not the point. In reality, both through Abraham ("through your seed—not seeds of many but one seed, Jesus's) and through Elijah, God is sowing into the earth what He wants to receive from the earth. Through Abraham He sows a lineage through which the Christ-child will come. Through Elijah, He sows a fathering spirit, through which the Lord would restore sons to the Father's house.

For unto us a child is born, and unto us a Son is given.

Isaiah 9:6

Why did the Father give a Son? Because He always gives first what He expects in return. He doesn't ask for it because He lacks it, but because something is purposed to be the fulfillment of the Father's desire. It is the Father's joy to see us fulfilled as sons and manifesting His sonship in us. He is looking at us in the rearview mirror until we are standing up in the backseat of the convertible!

Choosing Supernatural Fathers

He said He's going to call for the prophet Elijah because Elijah had a fathering spirit. Elijah would call sons to himself and would mentor them and father them. Do you remember when he called Elisha, and Elisha said, "I must go and bury my father"? Well, his father wasn't dead yet. That means it could be years before Elisha followed the call. Elijah said, "What's that to me?" In other words, "I'm giving you an opportunity. You can choose a natural father, or you can choose a supernatural father." And Elisha broke his plow, burned it and followed Elijah. When Elijah was called up in the chariot of fire, what did Elisha yell out? He cried, "My father, my father!" He had not only enrolled in the school of the prophet; he'd become a son.

The same option is available for you and me today. We can either enroll in quest for best practices, knowledge, skill sets, or we can become sons and get everything the Father has for us. Yes, I believe in education and acquiring knowledge—we need to be able to communicate to the widest audience possible. But before you are a leader, a pastor, a husband, a doctor, lawyer or evangelist, you must be a son.

> **"I'm giving you an opportunity. You can choose a natural father, or you can choose a supernatural father."**

The ominous words closing the Old Testament are an anticipation of what is coming in the New—the introduction of a Son and an invitation for all to have a place in the Father's bosom. It's a place of sonship, not an orphanage. It's neither grabbing your inheritance early and squandering it on your bucket list, nor dutifully working your life away out in the father's fields. It's a place in the Father's house, where you belong; a place you can call home; a place where the glory of God is your dwelling place, not a place you visit on special occasion.

Elijah had an anointing on him to gather and to raise sons, and for those sons to know that sonship. The schools of the prophets were all about the fathering spirit, and that spirit of the father would "turn the hearts of the fathers to the children, and the hearts of the children to their fathers, lest [the Lord] come and strike the earth with a curse" (Malachi 4:6). This global spirit of mistrust between the Father and His children was ambushed by a perfectly obedient Son who would only do the will of His Father. This Son would invite us all to call His Father our Father, His *Abba* our *Abba* (Matt 6:9). This Son submits even to the death of the cross, saying "Not My will but Yours be done." Then He is raised by the Father from death and pours out the Spirit of Adoption upon the planet of orphans, inviting everyone to come.

But in all of that, the father of lies has had tremendous success keeping the sons of God feeling and thinking like orphans. How could this be?

Where Everybody Knows Your Name

The old sitcom *Cheers* was known more for its theme song than its humor or quality of content—partially because the song itself resonated with the heart's need for a home: *"Sometimes you want to go where everybody knows your name, and they're always glad you came; you want to be where you can see, our troubles are all the same; you want to be where everybody knows your name."* The so-sad-that-it's-funny scenario featured all the lonely people who would rather be at the bar than at home. It makes one wonder how bad it must have been at home!

Have you ever had the nagging feeling that you don't belong; that you haven't found your group, or your "people"? Perhaps you wonder where you fit in—and find yourself with strangers. Perhaps you have experienced a tendency to move from one job to another, one church to another, one relationship to another .... The accusing voice of the orphan spirit seeks to keep uprooting us and moving us from place to place so that there is never a harvest for our labors.

The orphan spirit wants you to always be antagonistic to where God would set you. The orphan spirit never lets you settle in to sow seed, much less

The orphan spirit also causes us to resent the unchangeable qualities our lives.

enjoy the harvest on the down payment of your inheritance.

The orphan spirit also causes us to resent the unchangeable qualities of our lives. Those unchangeable features include our gender, the family in which we were born, the birth order between us and our siblings, physical features, mental intelligence features, and even our ethnicity, nationality, and place in history. In other words, the orphan spirit does not allow us to feel at home in our own skin. When we live in regret or resentment about those unchangeable features, we will always feel that we have been cheated, have the deck stacked against us, and ultimately will live in a low-grade bitterness toward God. After all, who made the determinations about our "unchangeable features" if it wasn't God?

If it seems you have heard this before, you have. It reminds me of the story of the guy sitting in the back of the church, listening to the preacher rehearse the woes of the world; when he had heard enough he called out, "Show us the cure, preacher. Show us the cure!" The good news is, there is a cure and Jesus came to show us how to move from curse to cure. Understanding that the spirit of sonship is received by revelation, through a life-long process of the *Abba Cry*, there are some things we can do to partner with His transformative work.

Five steps to move from Orphan to Heir

1. Forgive authorities where they have misrepresented the Father's love.

It begins with this—and this is absolutely non-negotiable. It starts with our own parents. Many of us don't even want to go there; we don't want to think about it or talk about it. We don't recognize the human tendency to cover for our parents by saying, "They did the best they could." And it is probably a true statement, but it doesn't deal with the wounds and scars we wear in our hidden emotions. We've settled those things, made up our minds, and it's done.

For some of us, one or both of our parents have already gone to be with the Lord, and we say, "I can't deal with that right now." But we can, because you can forgive in your own heart. If the enemy's plan is to get you to focus on the failures and the faults of those that were representing the Father's love in your life, then our first step toward sonship is to forgive those who misrepresented the Father's love. This may have started with your parents. No doubt it did. They loved you more than you knew, as every parent knows that you love your children more than they have the capacity to return that love because they came from your very flesh. (Our children cannot understand our love for them until they have children of their own).

The first step is to forgive those authorities—whether it's a parent, a pastor, or teacher—someone who was placed in your life to represent Father's love to you. Out of the brokenness of their human nature, out of their own orphan spirit, they messed up and now you're living in the bondage of that woundedness. I need to remind you that many times our authorities, our parents, our pastors, our leaders are communicating a conventional wisdom that's really nothing more than a culturally-acceptable languaging of their own woundedness. It falls short of an accurate representation of Father's love, and we must receive grace to forgive.

2. Seeking forgiveness and restitution from those you've wounded.

You may need to seek forgiveness and restitution. It may require going back to a parent, and saying "I was a 'hell on wheels' in this house." I, as a second-born son, have had to go back to my parents on numerous occasions and tell them,

"I'm just now realizing how much of a jerk I was while growing up. It took me a long time to realize how much pain I caused you. It never dawned on me when I went away to college that mom might want to hear from me every once in a while. It never dawned on me that mom might want me to pick up a phone and call her or write her a note telling her I missed her. When I left home, I left home! And it was some time later until I began to realize how painful that must have been. And when I had sons and daughters in college, and I was thankful that on rare occasion I received a text message telling me I was missed and loved, and all is well."

You may have to go back and seek forgiveness. You may have to go back and repay where damage has been done where your orphan spirit cost somebody something. I have had to seek forgiveness so many times that I truly feel like a professional "repenter." And that may never change. But you must know that the Father is not seeking punishment, but wholeness. Whatever the price, it's well worth it to experience the Father's pleasure, find the wholeness, and to enjoy the Father's smile on your life.

3. Live in Submission: We must acknowledge our need to be sons and daughters to someone.

In certain circles there has been conversation about spiritual fathers and the apostolic nature of raising up kingdom-leaders. We must learn that there won't be fathers until there are sons. Until somebody learns to submit to others, there are no fathers. This sounds backwards. It seems that fathers come first and sons as a result. But fathering cannot be forced on sons. A son must submit to a fathering spirit. But when we choose to be sons, we realize that the goal is not being great leaders; the goal is not being great mentors, the goal is not even to be great spiritual fathers. The goal is to be a son that always pleases the Father. Then we're willing and quick to find someone that we can get under and help them fulfill the Father's mission for them. And whether it's in business, or it's at home, or in your church or your education, you'll find that success comes when, in a spirit of sonship, you submit yourself and then help somebody else succeed. Then it becomes Father's pleasure to lift you up.

We often quote the Hebrew writer to say, "Looking unto Jesus, the author and finisher of our faith ..." to say, imitate Jesus. "WWJD," what would Jesus do? But why are we to look at Jesus? Because when we see Him we will see the obedient Son who never takes His eyes off His Father.

Have you ever been downtown among the skyscrapers and seen someone standing on the corner looking up? What happens? Everyone starts looking up to see what the person is looking at! When we look at Jesus we will see the Son looking up; His gaze fixed on the Father, saying:

> *I only do what I see my Father doing ... My Father is always working and I am always working.*
>
> John 5:17, 19

That is the spirit of sonship.

4. Be clothed in humility and patience: Sonship is more posture than position.

When we come to the place where our relationship with *Abba* is not based on our striving, works or merit, then we say what Paul said:

*This is not of ourselves, because everything we've received, we received
not of ourselves or of our own abilities, but we received from Him;
therefore our boasting is in the Lord.*
2 Corinthians 3:5

This is called "humility." It's the opposite of pride.

Patience is also a powerful by-product of the *Abba Cry*—the working of sonship in our hearts. One of the primary hooks that the enemy tries to use in my life is impatience and pride. I want to do it now; it has to happen, and it has to happen my way. Our society supports impatience. But when you find out that you are the Father's son and nothing happens to sons by accident, then you can glory in the fact that He's fulfilling His will and plan for your life. Yes, you're faithful. Yes, you're a good steward of what He puts in your hands. Yes, you take good care of those things He gives you to take care of. But really, the performing of it is by His power. We can say:

We work out our own salvation with fear and trembling.
Philippians 2:12, paraphrased

And yes, we have responsibility; but the next verse says the power comes from God (the Holy Spirit) working within us:

[Not in your own strength] *for it is God Who is all the while
effectually at work in you* [energizing and creating in you the
power and desire], *both to will and to work for His good pleasure
and satisfaction and delight.*
Philippians 2:13 (AMP)

If we will deal with our depth, He establishes the breadth of our lives. The reason patience becomes an overflow of the Spirit's work within me is that I come to realize I don't have to worry about the timing. If I'm His son, and if I put my life in His hands—focus on His pleasure— then His timing is right. All of my striving to stir something up, to make it happen, will probably only produce an Ishmael. Humility and patience is the posture of sons, because we know "our Father knows what we need even before we ask."

5. Cultivate the Presence of God as though it were your sole source of oxygen.

We were made for the Presence of God. Our spirit thrives in the Presence. When it's all said and done, the tangible difference between those that know God and those that don't, is the Presence. In His presence is fullness—of righteousness, peace, and joy in the Holy Spirit. We have too often settled for a weekly worship "experience" as though we still live in the Old Testament—needing to make our way to the Temple—when the Presence has taken up His home in us. We are to cultivate the Presence of God up from our spirits into our environment by singing songs, hymns, spiritual songs, making melody from our hearts to the Lord (Col. 3:16; Eph. 5:19).

What if spiritual disciplines are really doorways through which we release the Presence of God that is already in us? Spiritual disciplines of Christianity have long been promoted as a means whereby the believer can "get closer to God," as though God was happy with some distance. But what if prayer, worship, feeding on the Scriptures, fellowship with one another, communion, and fasting, were not actually about trying to get closer to God, but ways in which we cultivate (stir up) His presence and give it away?

If we begin to understand spiritual disciplines as "encounter triggers" whereby we meet God by the manifest presence of the Spirit, then we are not twisting God's arm for an answer, we are immersing ourselves in who He is. And this is what I know: the surest way and most direct path of transformation from an orphan spirit to sonship, is to hear the Father's voice (by the Spirit). Spiritual disciplines are simply a positioning ourselves to hear the Father speak to us, *"You are My beloved son/daughter; in you I am well pleased."*

What if spiritual disciplines are really doorways through which we release the Presence of God that is already in us?

Much has been said and written about practicing the presence of God. Suffice it to say here that it is difficult to conceive of any believer that walks in a revelation of the reality of their sonship that does not learn the importance of the abiding presence of God. It is by that abiding presence that Jesus did what He did (Acts 10:38), and that we are empowered as sons to do "these same works" (John 14:12-14).

Do you see a necessary sequential progression of these five steps? Forgiveness, restitution, submission, and humility are precursors, though not mutually exclusive, to welcoming and cultivating the Presence of God.

Returning to The Red Mustang and The Crucial Question

We began this journey looking into a red Mustang convertible, and a happy father driving through some of the most scenic terrain in North America. The scene is somewhere in Southeast Colorado in early summer– driving through a spacious landscape of lush, green pastureland– the mountains still snow-peaked in the distance on the right, and a crystal-clear river running with that "clear Rocky Mountain spring water" on the left. There are some cattle grazing in the open pastures, and an occasional farm house in the distance.

What is interesting in this prophetic scene is that each of the family members is doing something different. The father is driving with a sense of deep pleasure, clearly enjoying the opportunity to bring his family to such a beautiful place. His wife, however, is preoccupied with her smart phone, calculating distance, the route, next stops, conscientiously concerned, but not enjoying the gorgeous surroundings.

In the back seat is one daughter that seems in a bit of pain, if not traumatized. She seems to have had some traumatic travel experience in the past that leaves her paralyzed with fear about this trip and can't wait to arrive at their destination. She is not seeing any of the mountains, green pastures or refreshing river.

On the other side of the backseat, behind the father, the fifteen-year-old son has detached himself from his family by submerging himself in a video game and headphones. This trip wasn't his idea, it's a "bummer" having to be with family anyway, and he hasn't looked up from his game since they backed out of the driveway a few hours ago.

But in the middle of the backseat is a eight-year-old daughter named Joy. She is standing up in the seat, arms stretched out wide, with 70-mile-per-hour-wind blowing through her wavy blonde hair. She is squealing with delight—taking in the majesty of the mountains, then giggling and pointing to the rushing river. She has been soaking up the breathtaking views for some time—glancing repeatedly to see her father's eyes in the rearview mirror, sharing her joy.

Which Seat Are You In?

The grand hope is to stir you to stand up in the back seat, stretch your arms out wide.

The question is—right now in your life, in this place in your journey—which seat are you in? You might say, "Well, if I was driving through something that beautiful I would be taking in the scenery and enjoying the view!" But this is the point.

The Father is taking you on a beautiful journey—He is bringing glorious wonders to your life on a daily basis. The question is, are you seeing it? Do you find yourself spending your energy trying to chart your course, being the captain of your fate? Are you missing the glory of what God is doing around you because you somehow believe the guy driving the car hasn't given enough thought to everything that is involved in this trip? Are you one of those who is trying to make it happen?

Or perhaps you have hunkered down in life, not really experiencing much, not seeing much—after all there are too many bad things that can happen, or that have happened! The world is a dangerous place, and after all, you have some stories to tell about how quickly it can go wrong.

Or perhaps you fit better in the seat of the detached brother. You might tend to think, "There are more advanced things to do than take in the scenery. This whole idea of grandeur and beauty is for artists and religious folks, and you need adrenaline, or hard facts."

This book has really been a call to connect to the Father; to be one who has caught the Father's gaze and experiencing the Father's call to purpose. The grand hope is to stir you to stand up in the back seat, stretch your arms out wide, and begin to experience all that Father has prepared for you—until you laugh again, cry again, dream again. Until you get so full of His splendor that you can't keep it to yourself; you have to tell somebody else about Him.

Which seat are you in? I have shared this prophetic picture with numerous audiences, and I've asked the same question—which seat are you in? And invariably I will have someone approach me later and say, "You know, I think I am actually in more than one seat." Some have said, "I think I'm sitting in all of those seats."

Why don't you begin a sonship exercise right now? It's an exercise about hearing the Father's voice. Ask Him to talk to you about which seat you are in most of the time. Are you the controller in the front passenger seat, trying to "make it happen," analyzing all the possibilities? Are you traumatized, paralyzed in the pains of the past, the shame of the past, the fears of what could go wrong? Are you detached from others, just pouring yourself into whatever it is you are into, but not seeing anything that God is doing around you? You may want to pray:

Abba Father, every good and perfect gift comes from You. Your thoughts toward me are all good and I know you want to connect to me as a son. Would you talk to me about what seat I am in? What do you want to say to me right now? I'm listening.

Here's What I Know

We know that the orphan spirit says, "I must achieve, perform, succeed, earn my way into the family. I don't belong here."

But if you have read this far, my friend, you know something is changing. What does this change look like for you? Where are you now? How do you see yourself differently than before?

The spirit of sonship says, "I belong. I don't have to perform to be loved. I don't have to promote myself—the Lord has made me for purpose and He will put me in my purpose. I am a son. I am a daughter. I have a Father, I have a home, I have an inheritance, which means the cupboard will never be bare. I will always have what I need, when I need to have it. The Lord has given me gifts to freely give to others. He has given me His Holy Spirit to continually download the Father's will, purpose, and mission in me. This Spirit connects me directly to the Father's voice. I will never be alone again. I will never be on my own again. I will never be left in the dark again. I will know what I need to know when I need to know it, because this indwelling Spirit leads and guides me into all truth and shows me things to come. As long as I stay full of this Spirit of Adoption I will have nothing to hide, nothing to lose, nothing to fear, and nothing to prove. Even when my circumstances look dire, I have need of nothing. I have learned, that whatever state I am in, with little or much, I am independent of my circumstances. Father prepares a table before me in the presence of my enemies."

Does this sound more like you? The Holy Spirit is fully committed to bring this to reality in your life.

What Have We Said?

He graces us to forgive authorities for misrepresentation of the Father's love; this is the first step to moving from orphan to an heir.

Just like Elijah to Elisha, the Lord is giving us an opportunity to choose natural fathers or supernatural fathers, natural ways or supernatural ways.

Seeking forgiveness and restitution from those whom you have wounded, and forgiving those who have wounded you opens the passage ways of the spirit for God to accelerate your transformation.

In this relational kingdom it's important to acknowledge our need to be sons and daughters to spiritual fathers and mothers.

Because our Father knows what we need and when we need it, living in sonship brings a clothing of humility, patience, and focused listening.

PRAYER

Dear Abba, I know that You will not ask anything of me that You don't first give to me. I thank You both for giving me what You desire, and for the eyes to see it when it comes. Thank You that You are faithful to finish the work that You have begun in me and will work it out until the Day of Jesus Christ (Phil. 1:6). Would You continue to displace anything of the orphan spirit that is in me (thoughts, memories, desires, mindsets) by the Spirit of Adoption, the Holy Spirit, working sonship to the deepest places in my being? And I am convinced of this very thing, that what I have committed to You, You will keep to the day I see You (2 Tim 1:12). Abba, I belong to You. I love you. May the Abba Cry continually rise from my heart to my last breath. Amen.

GROUP DISCUSSION

1. Why is it so important to forgive those authorities that have misrepresented Father's love?

2. Why are patience and submission such obvious indicators of sonship?

3. Explain the relationship of cultivating the Presence of God to an ongoing transformation toward sonship?

4. Where do you see yourself right now in the red Mustang convertible?

Epilogue

Sonship: From Infant to Weaned

A Practical Application of Sonship

The most often asked question by parishioners to pastors is "Will you pray for me to know the will of God?" I understand it, because I have had numerous situations, as you have, where I wanted to hear from God about the next step. What do I do next?

When my wife and I felt we were to relocate from Houston to Dallas, we began to pray and confer with one-another about what we were sensing from the Lord. Selling a home and relocating to a new city is no small matter. I have seen lots of folks take big leaps over the years, and not all turned out well. But fear can never be the foundation if one wants to walk with God.

First, we received a clear release from our current assignment. This was confirmed by conversations with those under whom we were serving at the time. Through a series of divine appointments and my wife hearing the Holy Spirit say "this is where you are to live," we made the move and began to offer our gifts freely in our new church home (I was teaching in the university as adjunct faculty). By the way, I have learned that until and unless the Lord bears witness of His plan with your spouse, you only proceed to your own hurt.

We offered our teaching and prayer gifts freely to the church. I must admit, my emotions would slide into impatience; "When is something going to happen?" I stayed suspended between the tension of soul and spirit—in my soul (mind, will and emotions), I wanted to do whatever I could do to get to the next place of certainty. But then I would go into my place of prayer in the mornings and I would know in my spirit, "freely you have received, freely give."

What I have learned over the years is that there is a difference between my "thinker" and my "knower." My thinker is my soul (mind, will and emotions); my "knower" is my spirit, the inner man, the hidden man/person of the heart (1 Pet. 3:4). Man's soul feels the urgencies of time and is prone to impulsiveness; it says, "If I don't do something right now I will lose out on the opportunity." But neither the Spirit of God nor the

Kerry Wood

regenerated spirit of man is time-bound or time-sensitive. Your inner man lives in the eternal now. In your inner being is the sense that God is working all things out for your good. This is what the Bible calls "peace which passes all understanding" (Phil. 4:7). When I pray in the Spirit, wait upon the Lord in quietness, the peace from my spirit rises up and quiets my mind and soul.

David learned this lesson in his many times of waiting on God. He likened himself to a weaned child that doesn't have to cry and scream every time he gets hungry or needs a change:

Surely I have calmed and quieted my soul,
Like a weaned child with his mother;
Like a weaned child is my soul within me.

Psalm 131:2

What is the significance of being weaned? The child has now come to a place where he can communicate his needs in other ways. The weaned stage is a new stage of communication where a child can talk to his mother instead of just crying, forcing the mother to determine what the baby is trying to communicate.

This is a significant point in understanding the *Abba* Factor. Many believers never learn to develop their spirit man, or how to strengthen their spirit to have dominance over their soul/emotions. They only know to cry out like an infant, still on the mother's breast, anytime they have discomfort and don't know what is coming next. But by learning to commune with God, both with my mind and with my spirit (1 Cor. 14:15), the peace of God comes to rule like an umpire in my heart. Though my mind may not have the "what, when, and how" answers it is looking for, my spirit is at rest. I can know in my "knower" even if I can't explain it with my "thinker."

The Lord is constantly peeling layers of orphan thinking from our lives. The Lord is constantly revealing some impatience in me. The Lord is showing me places where I want to make something happen, and I want to stir something up, and I want to kick some doors down if they don't open. And it's all flesh; it's orphan spirit, but He is so gentle and patient in me, for me.

Patience is not the fruit of my best efforts; patience is a fruit of the Spirit's work in my life. With patience possess your soul. With patience I can harness the demands for immediate answers that come from my

160

emotions. As strange as it may sound, I have come to a place where I don't have to know the will of God. Jesus, by the Spirit, is the will of God in me, and I'll know what I need to know when I need to know it. I have found a new place of rest, like a weaned child. I can be Jesus to the world around me.

At one point during this most recent adventure, settling into our new place of ministry, the Lord spoke a word of deep comfort in my spirit. He said, *"Kerry, I am not keeping you from these things (opportunities), I am protecting you from things that will not be the best for you."* And now, in hindsight, I can see how right and loving He was in His guidance for us. How often we jump in quickly, driven by an impatient soul, demanding our orphan right to know (crying like a baby still on the breast), only later wishing we had waited a little longer.

Do you want to come to a place where you don't have to know the next step—you can quietly trust? Would you like to walk with me in a journey to say, "I want to be a son; I want to please the Father; I only want to say what the Father says, and do what I see the Father do"? It sounds like religious talk, but the Holy Spirit can take these things and make them real in our hearts until we hear coming up from our spirit, "Daddy! Father! In Your presence is where I want to be!" Let's go deeper.

> *For as many as are led by the Spirit of God,*
> *these are the sons of God.*
>
> Romans 8:14

Sonship is a place of rest. Sonship is a place of inheritance. Sonship is a place of knowing that it's not up to me, but to Father. My main priority is to hear the Father's voice and walk with Him. To go deeper check out *THE ABBA FORMATION.*

Endnotes

[1] Trish and Jack Frost, *Spiritual Slavery to Spiritual Sonship: Your Destiny Awaits You* (Shippensburg, PA: Destiny Image, 2006). My friend, Doug Stringer, gave me the CD series years ago and it put me on a quest.

[2] Jack W. Hayford, *Rebuilding the Real You: The Definitive Guide to the Holy Spirit's Work in Your Life* (Lake Mary, FL: Charisma House, 2009).

[3] Jesus did not come to reinforce the already wrong notions about God set in concrete by religion. He actually came to challenge and transform the primary notions Israel (and the world) had adopted of God as a judgmental, rule-keeping, sadistic God that enjoyed inflicting pain on humanity. Jesus also reinterpreted and transformed what priesthood, rabbinical ministry, law and covenant had come to mean. One must be careful not to use the rabbinical, religious notions of that day to try to understand who Jesus was; He came to reshape and redefine it, not to be understood by it.

[4] References to God as father in the Old Testament: Mal. 2:10; Ps 103:13; Jer. 3:4, 19; Mal. 1:6, Is 63:15; 64:8; Hos. 11:3, 8; Jer. 31:9, 20. These references show that God is father to those who do His will as well as to the individual Israelite.

[5] Joachim Jeremias, *The Central Message of the New Testament* (London: SCM Press, 1965).

[6] Jeremias says, "By the authorization that they, too, may invoke God as Abba, he lets them participate in his own communion with God. He even goes so far as to say that only he who can repeat this childlike 'Abba' shall enter the kingdom of God. This address, 'Abba', when spoken by the disciples, is a sharing in the revelation, it is actualized eschatology. It is the presence of the kingdom even here, even now. A fulfillment, granted in advance, of the promise. Ibid., 28-29.

[7] Raymond Brown, "The Death of the Messiah" as quoted by Gerald O'Collins, *The Tri-personal God* (New York: Paulist Press, 1999), 183.

[8] *"Abba"* as the nature of Jesus's relationship with the Father reveals what is behind the Kerygma (the disciples' message). This is more than a spin on the way the disciples wanted people to remember Jesus. We are confronted with something new and unheard of which breaks through the limits of Judaism. Here we see who the historical Jesus was: the man who had the power to address God as Abba and who included the sinners and publicans in the kingdom by authorizing them to repeat this one word, *"Abba,* dear Father."

[9]Jeremias says, "The evidence for the Christological statement about our adoption as sons and daughters is provided by the indwelling Spirit and the Spirit's use of the Son's language, "Abba, Father!" The indwelling of the Spirit is the way that both Father and the Son are present in the believer's life." Jeremias, 66-67.

[10]You Tube, "Funeral of Yasser Arafat," https://www.youtube .com/ watchtv f4lTa72glh0.

[11]The U.S. Committee for Refugees and Immigrants had the best article on this, but it has since been removed from their site. Tony Horowitz's Bagdad Without a Map treats this idea, though it is moving away from the purpose and topic of this book.

[12]"The Case for Christ" is a 2017 American Christian drama film directed by Jon Gunn and written by Brian Bird, based on a true story that inspired the 1998 book of the same name by Lee Strobel. The film stars Mike Vogel, Erika Christensen, Faye Dunaway and Robert Forster, and follows an atheist journalist who looks to disprove his wife's Christian faith. The film was released on April 7, 2017 by Pure Flix Entertainment.

[13]Lee Strobel, *A Case for Grace* (Grand Rapids: Zondervan, 2015), 20.

[14]Doug Wead, *The Raising of President and All the Presidents' Children* (Atria Books, 2005). Doug Wead chronicles that many other American Presidents lost their fathers at an early age. James Garfield was one year old when his father died. Andrew Johnson was three, Herbert Hoover six, George Washington eleven, and Thomas Jefferson fourteen. Fully nineteen presidents lost their fathers before they reached age thirty.

[15]Thanks to my friend Ryan Northcutt for this narrative connection.

[16]I've been saying this for years, "The greatest freedom is having nothing to hide, nothing to lose, nothing to fear and nothing to prove." I remember it as something that morphed from "The greatest liberty is having nothing to prove," by Pete Cantrell; quoted in R.T. Kendall, *The Anointing: Yesterday, Today, Tomorrow* (Lake Mary: Charisma House, 2003), 33.

[17]Are we saying that sonship is more important than salvation? One opens the door to the other, of course. But where we think of salvation as healing, wholeness and a ticket to heaven, sonship is an eternally unfolding destiny and purpose after you get there.

[18]The general structure of these twelve steps come from Trish and Jack Frost, *Spiritual Slavery to Spiritual Sonship: Your Destiny Awaits You* (Shippensburg, PA: Destiny Image, 2006). I owe the foundation of these thoughts to them, though I have modified them slightly over the years.

[19]"Sigmund Freud's Father Story," PBS.org, http://www .pbs.org/ youngdrfreud/pages/family_father.htm.   Devillier   Donegan Enterprises. 2002.

[20]Steven Beschloss, *The Gunman and His Mother: Lee Harvey Oswald, Marguerite Oswald and the Making of an Assassin* (Kindle Books: Media Wave, 2013).

[21]Bill Gaither, *I Am Loved.* Copyright 1982 Word Music, LLC; William J. Gaither, Inc.

[22]Thanks to Kevin Williams, friend and editorial reader, for this cogent thought.

[23]This story is a compilation of several churches and pastors I have met around the world. In Russia, the Republic of Georgia, Bogotá, Colombia, and even New Orleans, Louisiana, I met pastors that affirmed their flock like this, and members who would greet me and each other with a kiss on one check or both cheeks. The world is full of believers who are living in the freedom of the Father's love which creates child-like trust and vulnerability. I long to see it in all of God's people.

[24]Jeremy S. Sherman, "How to Need Less Affirmation" *Psychology Today,* August, 26, 2015.

[25]Stevie Wonder, "Don't You Worry About a Thing." Motown Records: Album, Innervisions; 1973.

[26]Henry Nouwen, *"Being the Beloved,"* a message preached at The Crystal Cathedral, Hour of Power, 1992.

[27]For greater insight on this matter, see Chiqui Wood's book, *Lessons Learned in the Battle* (Bedford, TX: Burkhart Books, 2015).

[28]Theodicy is the study of the origin of evil, which is not the purpose of this book. It is generally understood that bad things happen in a broken world for two primary reasons. First, under this curse of sin, Satan is temporarily the god of this world and influences demons, men, and to some degree creation. Secondly, man's free-will and the imperfection of anything man-made (airplanes, cars, buildings, etc.) can be the primary cause of tragedy. If a pilot fails to monitor his gauges and runs out of fuel, the plane crashes and those onboard die. This is a combination of human error and physics (gravity). To say that either God or the devil caused the crash could be considered superstitious. The point is that Satan plays on the pain and trauma of our tragedies and wounds to build strongholds.

[29]"See the Appendix article "Like A Weaned Child" for more distinction between spirit and soul.

[30]The original word translated as "transformed" (Rom 12:2) and "transfigured" (Matt. 17:2; Mark 9:2) is *metamorpheo*, which gives us a clue that the kind of transformation Paul speaks of here (and Jesus experiences on the Mount of Transfiguration) is much more than an intellectual exercise. See my book The Abba Formation (Burkhart Books, 2018) for more on the spiritual genesis of renewing the mind.

[31]God's promises, according to Hebrews 6:15-17, are based on the immutability of His counsel, where He swears by Himself since there is no one greater power to swear by. In covenant terms this means "if I ever fail to do what I have said, I will destroy myself." Of course, this is not possible to our understanding—God "cannot lie" and cannot self-destruct. His promises are that certain.

[32]My friend, Rabbi Ralph Marowitz, says the proper translation for Psalm 121:1 is not "to the hills" but "above the hills" because the idol worship was conducted at the tops of the hills, and David wouldn't have said, "I lift my eyes to the idols," but actually asserts the contrast, "I will lift my eyes above the hills... that's where my help comes from... from the Maker of Heaven and earth."

[33]Trevor Hart, "Humankind in Christ and Christ in Humankind: Salvation as Participation," *Scottish Journal of Theology* vol. 42, 72.

[34]Clark H. Pinnock, *Flame of Love* (Downers Grove: IVP, 1996), 21, 50.

Bibliography

Beschloss, Steven. *The Gunman and His Mother: Lee Harvey Oswald, Marguerite Oswald and the Making of an Assassin.* Kindle Books: Media Wave, 2013.

Frost, Trish and Jack. *Spiritual Slavery to Spiritual Sonship: Your Destiny Awaits You.* Shippensburg, PA: Destiny Image, 2006.

Hart, Trevor. "Humankind in Christ and Christ in Humankind: Salvation as Participation." Scottish Journal of Theology, 42.

Hayford, Jack W. *Rebuilding the Real You: The Definitive Guide to the Holy Spirit's Work in Your Life.* Lake Mary, FL: Charisma House, 2009.

———. *A Passion for Fullness.* Waco: Word Pub., 1990.

Jeremias, Joachim. *The Central Message of the New Testament.* London: SCM Press, 1965.

Kendall, R.T. *The Anointing: Yesterday, Today, Tomorrow.* Lake Mary: Charisma House, 2003.

Nouwen, Henry. *Life In The Beloved: Spiritual Living in a Secular World.* New York: The Crossroads Publishing Co., 1992.

O'Collins, Gerald. *The Tri-personal God.* New York: Paulist Press, 1999.

Pinnock, Clark H. *Flame of Love.* Downers Grove: IVP, 1996.

Polo-Wood, Chiqui. *Lessons Learned in the Battle: How to Live in Victory No Matter What.* Bedford, TX: Burkhart Books, 2015.

Sherman, Jeremy S. *"How to Need Less Affirmation."* Psychology Today, August, 26, 2015.

Strobel, Lee. *A Case for Grace.* Grand Rapids: Zondervan, 2015.

Wead, Doug. *The Raising of President and All the Presidents' Children.* Atria Books, 2005.

Wood, Chiqui. *The Abba Foundation.* Bedford, TX: Burkhart Books, 2018.

Wood, Kerry. *The Abba Formation.* Bedford, TX: Burkhart Books, 2018.

———. *The Gifts of the Spirit for a New Generation.* Zadok Publishing, 2015.

About the Author

Kerry Wood is passionate about authentic Christianity lived in the power of the Spirit. In over thirty-five years of pastoral ministry he has focused on the local church, prayer movements, and community transformation initiatives. He has launched or sponsored several church plants in the U.S. and abroad and has spoken in leadership conferences, crusades, and local churches in more than twenty countries and throughout the U.S. He has authored a variety of ministry materials, published articles, Bible curricula- and audio-video teaching.

As a local church leader, seminary professor and member of the Society of Pentecostal Studies, Kerry is committed to partnership with Holy Spirit, intercessory prayer, teaching the Word, five-fold equipping of the Church, leadership development and church planting. He endeavors to steward partnership with the Holy Spirit through the gifts, and introducing people to Spirit Baptism. His philosophy of life and ministry is about 'being' before 'doing', an overflow of God's fullness as the source of all activity.

Kerry holds a Doctor of Ministry and Master of Divinity from The King's University (Los Angeles), a Masters of Arts in Biblical Literature from the Assemblies of God Theological Seminary, and Bachelors in Christian Ministry from Southwestern Assemblies of God University.

Kerry is married to (Dr.) Ana (Chiqui) Wood, and has four grown children, Robert, Geoffrey, Audrea, and Lauren.

www.DrKerryWood.com

www.TableofFriends.com

Check out the other two books in the trilogy:

THE ABBA FOUNDATION:
True freedom from the orphan spirit is impossible
without a right view of God.

THA ABBA FORMATION:
Do you want to go deeper? Learn to partner with Holy Spirit who searches the Father's heart and discloses His purposes to you through spiritual words.